MW01154649

THROUGH
FOUR SEASONS

Books by
Edith M. Patch

NATURE STUDY
Dame Bug and Her Babies

Hexapod Stories

Bird Stories

First Lessons in Nature Study

Holiday Pond

Holiday Meadow

Holiday Hill

Holiday Shore

Mountain Neighbors

Desert Neighbors

Forest Neighbors

Prairie Neighbors

NATURE AND SCIENCE READERS
Hunting

Outdoor Visits

Surprises

Through Four Seasons

Science at Home

The Work of Scientists

THROUGH FOUR SEASONS

by

Edith M. Patch and

Harrison E. Howe

illustrated by

Eleanor O. Eadie

and

Mary L. Morse

YESTERDAY'S CLASSICS

ITHACA, NEW YORK

Cover and arrangement © 2018 Yesterday's Classics, LLC.

This edition, first published in 2018 by Yesterday's Classics, an imprint of Yesterday's Classics, LLC, is an unabridged republication of the text originally published by The Macmillan Company in 1933. For the complete listing of the books that are published by Yesterday's Classics, please visit www. yesterdaysclassics.com. Yesterday's Classics is the publishing arm of the Baldwin Online Children's Literature Project which presents the complete text of hundreds of classic books for children at www. mainlesson.com.

ISBN: 978-1-63334-102-9

Yesterday's Classics, LLC
PO Box 339
Ithaca, NY 14851

A LETTER TO THE GIRLS AND BOYS

Dear Girls and Boys:

You are the same children all through the year, but you do not look just the same in winter and in summer. Your January clothes are different from those you wear in July. Perhaps the color of your skin is changed, too. It will be a few shades darker during the season of brightest sunshine if you are outdoors as much as you should be. You may have more freckles in summer, and perhaps your hair will be bleached by the sun to a little different shade.

People do not do exactly the same things in spring as they do in the fall. Farmers plant seeds in the ground in the spring. In the fall they harvest food for winter use. Storekeepers show different things in their shop windows in summer and winter.

Fashions change in games as well as in work. You like to play some games in summer that would not be nearly so pleasant in winter.

People may be happy at any time in the year, and yet there is some difference in the kinds of happiness. The joy you have in looking at the first pussy willow or bluet or violet or other spring flower is not quite the same as that you feel in the jolly fall, when the chattering squirrel gathers his acorns and the trees let their gay leaves go fluttering down.

If people do not look and act and feel just the same at different times of the year, what about the rest of the world?

Well, a bobolink is the same bird in the fall as he is in the spring, although he does not look and act the same. In the spring he wears a suit of white and black and yellow, but in the fall his feathers show mostly olive and brown colors. He does not act the same, either. In the spring he sings a joyous bubbling song of many lovely, lively notes. In the fall he repeats, over and over again, one call that sounds as if he were answering the rest of the bobolinks, who are all making the same sociable sound.

You will understand that there is not room in one book to tell about more than a few of the wonderful things in the world, for a book is small and the world itself is very large. There are indeed more interesting things in the world than have ever been described in all the books that have been printed.

So suppose that you read the chapters in this book and think about them in a special way. Think about them as samples of what the world has to show. Then perhaps you will wish to look at the things of the world for yourselves.

We wish you happy hours—all through the year.

Your friends,

EDITH M. PATCH
HARRISON E. HOWE

CONTENTS

SPRING

SUMMER

AUTUMN

CHAPTER I

A WILD APPLE TREE IN FALL

An apple tree lived at the edge of some woods. It was called a wild apple because no person had planted it or taken care of it or given a name to the sort of apples it bore.

The tree grew from a seed that had been dropped near the woods more than sixty years ago. Would you like to guess how the seed was dropped? Nobody really knows, but of course anyone may guess about it.

Perhaps a crow picked the apple the seed was in and flew with it toward the woods. A crow has a funny way of picking apples. He flies very slowly to the end of a branch and takes the stem of the apple in his bill. He carries the fruit by the stem to some place he likes for a picnic ground. Then he makes joyful cawing chuckles as if he were rather pleased with himself, as no doubt he is.

Or it may be that some boy or girl about your age threw away an apple core while walking near the woods one fall day years ago. And perhaps the wild apple tree grew from one of the seeds in that core.

When the tree was old enough, it had apples every year. Some wild apples are hard and sour and bitter. Others are quite as good to eat as any apples that grow in orchards. The apples on the tree at the edge of the woods had pretty red skins and a delicious taste.

No man did anything for this wild tree, but it had some care in other ways.

Often a little bird with a black cap came and sang among its branches. He came during the summer, when many other birds also visited the tree. He came, too, in the fall, after most other birds had gone south. His name was Chickadee.

His name was Chickadee.

Chickadee took a great deal of exercise. Perhaps

that is why he had so good an appetite. He was nearly always hungry.

He did not eat any of the bright red apples, though. He never did seem to care for juicy fruits. But he found something else on the branches that he liked. He found some oyster-shell scales with eggs under them.

An oyster-shell scale is a tiny, dark brown object that is shaped somewhat like an oyster shell. It is larger at one end and curved. It is made with a sort of wax.

The insect that makes such a scale has parts in its body that are called wax glands. The wax that is formed in the glands is so soft that it can be pushed out through openings (pores) in the insect's body. But after the wax has been pushed out where the air touches it, it becomes hard. It is then a shiny shell-like covering for the insect. When the insect molts, its old skin is added to the scale.

This little insect lays all its eggs under the waxen scale that covers its body. Often there are more than fifty eggs under one scale. They stay under the scale all winter. That is, they do unless something happens to them.

Perhaps you know that a chickadee likes insect eggs. So between his songs he helps himself to what he finds under the oyster-shell scales.

A full-sized scale of this sort is only about one eighth of an inch long. So you can be sure that the fifty or more eggs it covers are very, very small. They are, indeed, so tiny that a chickadee can eat hundreds of them and still be hungry enough to hunt for more.

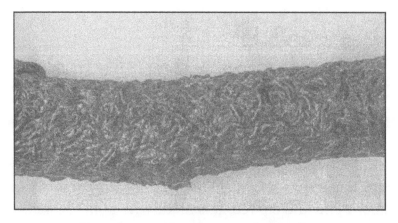

Branch covered with oyster-shell scales

Oyster-shell scale insects harm trees by piercing the tender bark and sucking the juice. So the more of these eggs a chickadee eats, the better for the tree.

There were other kinds of eggs on the wild apple tree in the fall. When Chickadee tasted them, he felt so cheerful he sang.

He liked the tent-caterpillar eggs, for one kind. Of course tent caterpillars did not lay the eggs, for no caterpillar can lay an egg. But tent caterpillars hatch from such eggs in the spring unless something happens to them before that time.

A reddish brown moth lays tent-caterpillar eggs in the summer. She puts three or four hundred eggs in one mass. The mass is like a ring around the twig. The moth covers her eggs with a liquid that hardens in the air. So the egg mass has a waterproof cover. It looks like shiny varnish with tiny bubbles in it.

Chickadee could pick through the waterproof cover with his strong little bill. And it was well for the apple tree that he could find the eggs, for tent caterpillars eat apple leaves. A tree can spare some of its leaves very well, but it needs most of them itself.

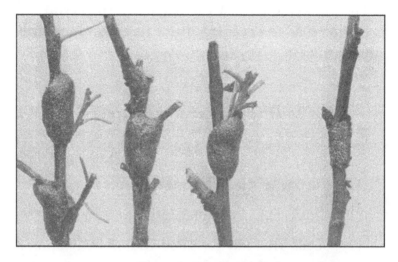

Egg masses from which tent caterpillars hatch

In one way and another the wild apple tree gave much pleasure during the fall days. It furnished rosy apples to boys and girls and crows that came to pick some of them. Some of the fruit fell to the ground and supplied many picnic dinners to crickets and other little six-footed creatures.

A pretty striped chipmunk came for some seeds and whistled in a shrill way whenever he was disturbed at his feast. A gay, chattering red squirrel went off with some of the apple seeds. And a quiet little meadow mouse ran that way, now and then, for his part of the treat.

The tree was a sort of storehouse, too, of insect eggs,

as you have read. Woodpeckers and nuthatches helped the chickadee eat them.

So when you think of the wild apple tree, which had no person to take care of it at all, perhaps you will feel rather glad to know that these three kinds of birds came to visit it.

What To Do after Reading Chapter One

READ

Choose one of the following subjects to read:

(1) "Chick, D.D.," Chapter I in *Bird Stories*.

(2) "Seeds That Pay for Their Rides," in Chapter 3 in *First Lessons in Nature Study*.

(3) "Juicy Fruits," in "Some Food from Plants" in *Surprises*.

WRITE

Choose one of the following subjects and write about it. Write at least fifty words.

(1) *Chickadee.* Tell something about this bird. Tell what kinds of food he likes. Tell how he can help take care of an apple tree.

(2) *Apple Seeds.* Apples that are left on a tree fall to the ground in time. There would not be room for young apple trees to grow under the branches of the old tree. Write about some different ways in which apple seeds

can be carried to places where they may find room to grow.

(3) *Rose Family*. The apple tree belongs to the Rose Family. If you chose to read "Juicy Fruits," tell about some other fruits that grow on plants of the Rose Family.

AN APPLE HUNT

If you live in the country, *look at* as many different kinds of apples as you can find on trees. Tell what colors you see on the ripe apples. *Do not touch* any apples unless the owner of the tree gives them to you. (Remember your outdoor good manners!)

If you live in the city, *look at* as many different kinds of apples as you can find in stores. Tell all the colors you can see on the ripe apples. If you buy an apple, you may like to show it to the boys and girls in your class.

AN APPLE SHOW

Ask your teacher if she would like you to have a little Apple Show in your room. Perhaps she will help you plan for one.

Looking at potato plants

CHAPTER II

HEALTHY POTATOES

Did you ever meet a plant doctor who spends his time looking at potatoes to see whether they are sick or healthy? Do you know how careful a farmer must be to keep his potato plants well?

Autumn is the time when potatoes are dug and stored for the winter. They should have smooth skins. Their flesh should be sound—without dark spots or streaks. They should, indeed, be healthy in the fall if they are to keep in good condition to eat during the winter, for sick potatoes are likely to rot or to become spoiled in other ways while they are lying in cellars or other storage places.

They must be well, too, if they are to serve as suitable seed potatoes in the spring.

Potatoes belong to the same plant family as tomatoes. A tomato plant has its seeds in fruits that grow in the flower clusters. So does a potato plant.

A man who wishes to have tomato plants in his garden grows them from seeds that are taken from ripe tomatoes. Potato plants, also, may be grown from seeds taken from ripe potato fruits.

However, for many good reasons, the farmer who grows potatoes for food does not plant potato seeds at all. He plants, instead, the potatoes themselves after he has cut them into suitable pieces. These are called seed potatoes or seed pieces, though there are no seeds in them. Potatoes have buds (often called "eyes"). Sprouts start from these buds and grow into new potato plants.

So you see that the farmer should have good sound seed potatoes to put away in the fall if healthy plants are to grow from them in the spring.

Even if the plants start from good potatoes, they may become ill later. Perhaps the plant doctor will come into the field and look at them and say, "These potatoes have *late blight.*"

Leaves from a potato plant that has late blight

Late blight is a disease caused by a kind of *fungus.*

Funguses (or *fungi*) have no flowers or leaves. They cannot get food from the air and the soil, as can plants with green leaves. They must take their food from other plants or from animals. A *toadstool*, or *mushroom*, is a kind of large fungus. Molds on jelly or old bread are kinds of small fungi.

The kind of fungus that causes late blight is so small that you cannot see one of these fungi without a magnifying glass. Late blight may make brown places on the potato leaves. It may attack the stems and the potatoes in the ground.

If a potato that is sick with late blight is planted, the new potato plants that grow from it are likely to have late blight, too. The stalks of such plants may be slender and weak.

As you have just learned, a fungus does not have flowers. It does not have seeds either. Instead of seeds, it has *spores*. The spores are very fine and blow about like dust.

Spores from the late-blight fungus may blow from sick leaves to well plants. They may be washed from the air on to plants by raindrops. So the disease may spread in damp weather. Sometimes whole fields of potatoes die from late blight.

Or the plant doctor may look at some potatoes and say, "They have *blackleg*." The base of the stem of a potato plant sick with this disease becomes quite black. The potatoes may have bad-smelling, rotten places.

Blackleg is caused by a kind of *bacterium*. A

This potato plant has blackleg.

bacterium is a tiny living thing. Its body consists of only one small part called a cell. (Two or more of these little forms of life are called *bacteria*.) Bacteria are so exceedingly small that hundreds of them could live in a drop no larger than the period at the end of this sentence.

Most kinds of bacteria are harmless. Many kinds are helpful to plants and animals. But some kinds cause diseases in plants or animals. Perhaps you know that *diphtheria* and *tuberculosis* are two kinds of diseases that bacteria may cause people to have.

There are still other kinds of potato diseases caused by fungi and bacteria. Late blight and blackleg are only two of them.

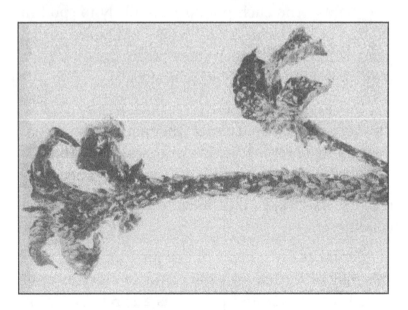

Aphids on potato stem and leaves

Sometimes plants become ill because *aphids* carry the juice of sick plants in their mouths and take it to well plants. Aphids are small insects with sharp, slender mouth parts. They thrust their beaks into leaves or stems of plants and suck the juices. If they feed on sick potato plants and later put their beaks into well plants, they may give the healthy plants some diseases in this way.

You do not need to worry about eating sick potatoes. You will not have late blight or blackleg or any other potato disease even if you taste potatoes from sick plants. People and potatoes do not have the same diseases.

Farmers, however, worry about the health of their potatoes. They cannot get good crops of potatoes from sick plants. And such potatoes are likely to spoil in storage. So the farmers read books and bulletins that plant doctors have written about potato diseases. Then they try to keep their potatoes healthy.

They begin by giving their seed potatoes a bath before they cut them into seed pieces. They put something into the bath that prevents certain diseases.

After the potato plants are growing in the field, the farmers spray or dust them to keep them in good condition.

Bordeaux is the name of one mixture that is used. This may be dusted over the plants in a dry form or mixed with water and put on as a spray. Bordeaux protects potatoes from late blight and some other diseases.

When a farmer wishes to get rid of the aphids on his potato plants, he is likely to use a poison with *nicotine* in it. Nicotine is found in tobacco. This poison is mixed with other things and put on the plants as a dry dust or used in a wet spray. Nicotine kills aphids in a short time; so this is a useful poison.

A power potato sprayer

Colorado potato beetles are sometimes so numerous in a field that they could eat enough leaves to cause the plants to die unless something was done to stop them.

A Colorado potato beetle has bright tan wing covers with ten black stripes on them. It shuts the wing covers down over its back like a hard shell when it is not flying. The shell-like covers protect the thin red wings.

Less than one hundred years ago there were no beetles of this kind anywhere in our country except in the West near the Rocky Mountains. They lived on wild plants belonging to the Potato Family. They had never tasted potato leaves. After people planted potatoes in that part of the country, the beetles began to eat them. Each year some of them flew from one field to a new one farther on, until at last they reached all parts of the country where potatoes are grown.

The beetles lay their yellow eggs in clusters on the plants. The fat, reddish, wingless young that hatch from the eggs eat potato leaves even more greedily than the old beetles do.

Colorado potato beetles

Farmers save their potatoes from these insects by spraying the plants with a poison that has *arsenic* in it.

The pests eat the sprayed leaves and die.

A promising field of potatoes

Even if there were no insects and no diseases to attack potato plants, farmers would need to be rather careful of this crop, for they have to keep the soil in good condition. Potatoes grow best in soil that is slightly acid, but not too acid. If the soil is too acid for the potatoes, *lime* must be added. Lime makes soil less acid. There must be, too, the right sort of plant food in the soil. Some food for plants is prepared in factories. It is one kind of *fertilizer*. Farmers often buy it and put it on the soil.

After the crop is dug, the potatoes must still have care. They must be stored in places that are cold enough, but not too cold.

So, in one way and another, potatoes need attention all through the year. When you taste a white baked potato that is so perfect that even the skin is good to eat, you may think of the farmer who took care of the crop. You may like to think, too, of the plant doctors who have learned so much about keeping potatoes healthy.

What To Do after Reading Chapter Two

A POTATO SHOW

If your teacher approves, have a Potato Show at school. Perhaps a few members of your class will offer to bring samples of potatoes for the show.

Choose one of your class to pretend he is a plant doctor. Let the plant doctor say which potatoes he thinks look as if they have smooth, healthy skins. Let him cut a few of the potatoes to see whether the flesh is firm and sound or whether it has dark spots or streaks.

READ

Choose at least one of the following subjects to read:

(1) *Aphids.* You have just read something about potato aphids. The story of another kind of aphid may be found in the chapter of *Holiday Pond* that is called "Nim Fay, the Sap-Drinker."

In Chapter 1 in *First Lessons in Nature Study* there is a section called "Aphids and Honeydew."

(2) *Beetles.* You have just read something about potato beetles. The story of another kind of beetle may be found in *Hexapod Stories* in the chapter called "Lampy's Fourth o' July."

(3) *Tubers.* Read "Tubers" in Chapter 3 in First Lessons in Nature Study.

ANSWER THREE QUESTIONS

Here are six questions. Answer any three of them.

(1) Does an aphid chew the leaves of a plant? If not, how does it feed?

(2) Tell two ways in which aphids may harm a plant.

(3) Look at the pictures of some aphids and some beetles. Then tell how the wings of an aphid differ from those of a beetle.

(4) Write a list of all the different kinds of beetles whose names you can remember.

(5) Tell one fact about each beetle in your list.

(6) Does a beetle chew food or suck it?

TUBERS, ROOTS, AND BULBS

White potatoes are called *tubers.* These tubers are thickened underground stems. Beets, carrots, and turnips are thickened roots. Onions, as you know, are thickened underground leaf buds or bulbs.

Look at a potato, a carrot (or beet or turnip), and an onion. Are there any roots on the potato tuber? Are there any "eyes" on the carrot or onion?

Cut a potato, a carrot, and an onion in halves. What differences do you find inside?

CHAPTER III

CORN

Sometimes the same name is given to several different things. The word *corn* does not always mean the same kind of grain. If a boy who lives in England says, "I ran through a cornfield," he means that he ran through a field of wheat or barley or oats or rye. But if a child who lives in this country says, "I ran through a cornfield," he means that he ran through a field of *maize* or *Indian corn*.

When people came from England to America, they found Indians raising maize. So they called it Indian corn.

Wheat, barley, oats, rye, and maize are some of the plants that belong to the Grass Family. Rice, too, belongs to the same family of plants. The seeds of these plants are grain that people use for food for themselves or for their horses and cows and some other animals. Such seeds are of great importance.

When the wheat crop is not good in some countries, the people suffer from hunger because they do not have bread enough. When the rice crop fails in China, many of the people there starve. But years when there

This cornstalk is more than sixteen feet tall.

is plenty of grain for food, the people are happy. It is time to rejoice when the ripe seeds have been gathered. There have been celebrations in the fall at harvest time for many hundreds of years in different countries. Sometimes you may hear such a celebration spoken of as a "feast of the ingathering at the end of the year."

In England, a long time ago, the old-time harvesters brought home the last bundles of grain very gaily every year. Some of the girls, in bright dresses, rode in the carts. Other reapers danced to the music of pipes. They sang:

> We have plowed, we have sowed,
> We have reaped, we have mowed,
> We have brought home every load,
> Hip, hip, hip, harvest home!

Our own national harvest festival in the United States of America is the holiday known as Thanksgiving Day.

Long before there were any white people in America to have Thanksgiving Day feasts, Indians had thankful celebrations. They did not have the kinds of corn known as wheat or barley or rye or oats. But they had their maize, which they loved. They told stories and sang songs about it in their own language. Some of these have been changed to English words, so that we can understand them. This is one of them.

AN INDIAN HYMN OF THANKS TO MOTHER CORN

See! The Mother Corn comes hither,
  Making all hearts glad!
Making all hearts glad!
Give her thanks, she brings a blessing;
  Now, behold! she is here!

Indian corn has been a very important crop for white people in this country ever since they learned about it from the Indians.

There are now many varieties of this kind of corn. Some kinds have white seeds, or kernels; others have yellow kernels; and still others have kernels that are nearly black.

The stalks of some kinds of corn grow taller than a man and have big ears. The stalks of some kinds are so short that you could reach their tops. They have small ears with little kernels that are used for pop corn.

You know that people eat sweet corn while the kernels are young and tender. Perhaps you like to nibble unripe kernels from a cob yourself. You may have eaten sweet corn that has been cut from the cobs and canned.

Sometimes kernels of ripe corn are soaked in something that loosens the *hull,* or horny outside covering. Then the loose hulls are rubbed off under water. Great quantities of such hulled corn are prepared and sold in cans. One name for it is *hominy*. Many people think it makes delicious porridge.

Coarse corn meal and fine corn flour are made from ripe, dry kernels that are heated and ground in mills. Such meal and flour are used in many kinds of food.

Some of the dry ground corn that is not used in the meal or flour is sold to farmers to feed their cows. It is called *hominy feed;* but of course it is not at all like the soaked hulled corn, called hominy, that makes good porridge.

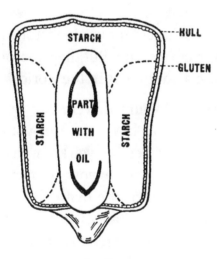

Inside the hull are gluten and starchy and oily parts.

Inside the tough, horny hull, there is a part of the kernel that has a great deal of starch. In the center of the starchy part, there is a smaller portion of the kernel that has oil in it. There is *gluten* between the hull and the starchy part.

A little more than half of the kernel is starch. This can be separated from the rest as tiny white particles. Starch does not dissolve in cold water. In hot water, however, it changes to a sticky substance. This sticky stuff can be used, as laundry starch, to make clothes stiff. Or it can be used, as cooking starch, to make food thick—like cornstarch pudding.

Hot sticky starch can be changed to a sweet syrup by adding a very little acid to it. The acid itself is sour, but it changes the starch to a good-tasting, sweet substance that is called *corn syrup*. Millions of bushels of corn are used every year for making this sweet syrup.

The acid that is added to the starch and hot water has a long name. It is called *hydrochloric acid*. This is a dangerous acid when it is strong. But when a very little of it is mixed with a great deal of water, it is useful to us in many ways.

People make hydrochloric acid for use in factories in changing cornstarch to corn syrup. But they do not make all the hydrochloric acid there is in the world.

You use hydrochloric acid yourself every day. But you do not need to buy it. You have some in your stomach. It is in your *gastric juice*. Perhaps you know that gastric juice helps your food to digest in your stomach. And would you like to know what the hydrochloric acid in your gastric juice does? It changes starch into sugar for you. So when you eat cornstarch in corn food, hydrochloric acid in your digestive juices helps change the starch to sugar. This acid does the same thing when you eat wheat starch in bread or rice starch in boiled rice or potato starch in cooked potatoes.

Starch food is important for you to eat. But your body cannot use the starch itself. The starch must be changed to sugar first. That is one way hydrochloric acid helps you.

The gluten of the kernel is used as *gluten meal.* The hull, or covering of the kernel, is ground into *bran.* A good kind of food for cattle is made by mixing gluten with bran.

The middle, oily part of the kernel is important, too. The best oil that is taken from this part is used for food. It may be eaten, instead of olive oil, with salads. It may be used, instead of butter or lard, in cooking. This maize oil is sold in stores. Oil from corn that is not good enough for food may be used in making soap or glycerin.

Fall is the time of year when you can find cornstalks cut and standing in the field. They are in bunches called *corn shocks.*

But the seeds of these plants are with you all through the year—in one form or another—for there are more than one hundred different products made from maize seeds and sold in stores. We have told you in this chapter about only a few of these many things. Can you find out what some of the others are?

Perhaps this fall you will visit a farm and run through a field of the kind of corn called maize. Perhaps you will hunt in one of the shocks for an ear of corn. Then what will you do? Will you take off the husk from the ear and look at the rows of kernels? Will you think of some of the things that can be made from the seeds of this wonderful plant that belongs to the Grass Family?

Three good ears of Indian corn

What To Do after Reading Chapter Three

A CORN SHOW

If your teacher is willing, have a Corn Show at school. Bring samples of the grain that boys and girls in this country call corn. Bring samples of the different kinds of grain that children in England call corn.

Let one member of the class bring an ear of unripe maize. It may be raw or cooked. Give each child one or more kernels. Find the hull. Find the starchy part. Find the oily central part.

Soak a dry ripe kernel of maize until it is soft enough for you to find these parts.

Bring pictures of different things that can be made from maize. These pictures may be part of the Corn Show.

READ

Read "Other Grains and Their Uses," Chapter 5 in *First Lessons in Geography*.

INDIANS AND PILGRIM FATHERS: A PLAY

As you have probably learned, the people of the first English colony that settled in Massachusetts are known as the Pilgrims. They sailed from Plymouth, England, in September and landed in Massachusetts in December. They did not have enough food to last them all winter.

The Indians let them have some of their corn.

Perhaps you will like to have a play in school. Some of you may pretend that you are the hungry men, women, and children of the early Massachusetts colony. Others of you may pretend that you are Indians coming with corn to give to the Pilgrims. Plan what the different players will do and say.

CHAPTER IV

EGGS IN COLD STORAGE

People put hens' eggs into cold places if they do not wish to use them soon after they are laid. Then the eggs remain good enough for food for a long time. We say that such eggs are in cold storage.

Tussock moths use cold storage for their eggs. A mother tussock moth puts her eggs on the outside of her cocoon soon after she comes out of it. The eggs stay there all winter. They are so cold that they cannot

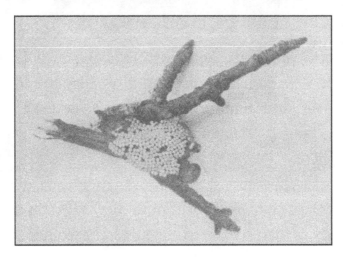

Eggs on a tussock moth's cocoon

Hens' eggs in cold storage

spoil or hatch. In the spring they are still in good condition. They hatch when the weather becomes warm enough. Then the young tussock caterpillars begin to eat leaves and grow.

Crickets use cold storage for their eggs. They do not leave their eggs exposed in the air, as tussock moths do. They poke holes in the ground and lay their eggs there. These eggs remain cool and fresh all through the winter months. The ground becomes warm in the sunshine when spring comes. Then the eggs hatch, and the young crickets come out of their little caves or cold cellars. They hunt for food and begin to grow.

There are many other kinds of insects that live through the winter in the egg stage. That is why there are so many young insects every spring.

Some kinds of fish, too, put their eggs into cold storage. Salmon do this.

Pacific salmon leave the Pacific Ocean and travel up fresh-water streams until they find good places to deposit their eggs. Atlantic salmon, also, leave salt water and seek suitable places in fresh water for their eggs. Sometimes people keep salmon eggs in hatcheries.

The salmon of the west coast and of the east coast both deposit their eggs in the fall. Their eggs do not hatch until the next spring, when the water becomes warmer. This cold storage does them no harm.

The Atlantic Ocean, you know, reaches all the way from North America to Europe. There are salmon, called Atlantic salmon, that travel up the rivers in England and

France and Norway and some other places in Europe. These are the same kind of fish that travel up some of the northern rivers in eastern United States and Canada.

Wherever salmon live, they must have fresh water for their eggs. That is why they go into rivers and lakes.

We say fish are *spawning* when they lay their eggs. The spawning season for the Atlantic salmon is in November, after most of the leaves have fallen from the broad-leaf trees.

A salmon is a beautiful fish most of the year. But during the spawning season it grows lank and changes its shape. Its fins become thick and its skin is slimy. A father salmon changes even more than a mother salmon does. His jaws become curved like hooks.

After the spawning season, the Atlantic salmon go back to the sea if they can get there. They live in salt water about half of the year.

But some salmon live in lakes from which they cannot escape to the sea. So they stay in fresh water all through the year. These fish are said to be *landlocked*, because they are locked away from the sea. Landlocked salmon do not grow so large as the salmon do that live part of the time in salt water.

The mother salmon seek shallow water when they are ready to lay their eggs. They go near the edges of lakes or into brooks that flow into the lakes.

Men have made pens, or pounds, in some lakes by driving long posts into the bottom of the lakes. They catch some of the salmon and put them into the pounds before they lay their eggs. The men in charge of these fish handle them carefully. They take the eggs and place them in fish hatcheries. These eggs are kept in very cold water until it is time for them to hatch. Then the water is kept as warm as the water in the lake in springtime when the sun is shining on it.

This building is a fish hatchery where salmon eggs are kept in cold storage.

Eggs of landlocked salmon are about the size of small peas. They look rather clear, like grains of cooked tapioca, but they have a pinkish yellow tint.

The picture on the next page was taken in November while the salmon were spawning near the edge of the lake. The fish that live in this lake are landlocked. Some of them are caught each fall and put into the pound. The eggs taken from these fish are cared for in a fish hatchery. The baby fish that hatch from the eggs are kept in the hatchery and fed until they are several months old. Then they are set free in different lakes and streams.

A salmon pound in a Maine lake

What To Do after Reading Chapter Four

USE A GLOBE

Look at a globe to find the location of the Atlantic and the Pacific oceans.

Find England and France and Norway. Find the United States. In the United States find Maine, the most northern state in the East. Find the state of Washington, in the West.

The Atlantic salmon is a rather northern fish. It does not travel very far south.

Why do you think the same kind of salmon (Atlantic salmon) go up the rivers of Maine and England and France and Norway?

Why do you think this same kind of salmon does not find its way to the rivers of Washington at spawning time? Where would it have to travel to get there?

READ

Read "How We Get Food from the Sea," Chapter 8 in *First Lessons in Geography.* Read about fish hatcheries on pages 207–209 in *Introduction to World Geography.*

HUNTING FOR FISH PICTURES

Look up the names of different kinds of fish in a dictionary (or encyclopedia) and see the pictures near them. Perhaps there is also a full page of pictures of fish among the pictures at the back of the dictionary.

Look for the picture of the salmon on that page. See how many fins the salmon has. Do some of the other fishes on that page have the same number of fins? Do some have a different number? Find a fish with fins that are different in shape from those of a salmon.

Look for some fish pictures in papers that are given you to cut up. If you find some good pictures, put them on a chart or in a scrapbook.

WRITE

Write four sentences, using in each sentence one of the following expressions:

(1) spawning season   (3) cold storage

(2) landlocked   (4) fish hatcheries

A monarch butterfly

CHAPTER V

GOING SOUTH

Many people stay in the same part of the country all through the year. But some people go north for the summer and south for the winter. They look across some northern hill in the fall. They see the crimson and scarlet and golden leaves of trees and bushes with, here and there, the steadfast color of evergreens. They know that before many weeks the red and yellow colors will be gone. Only the evergreens will show against the white snows of winter. So they make their plans to go south—by land or by water or by air.

Such travelers go because they choose and not because they must. They find it pleasant to be in different places during different times of the year. There are creatures, however, that travel at certain times because it is natural for them to do so. When the right time comes, they feel like going and so they go. This feeling is so strong that they cannot stay—it is stronger than a choice. It is a necessary part of their lives.

Most kinds of insects stay in the same region all through the year. But there are certain butterflies that leave the North and fly to the South, where they spend the winter months.

Monarch butterflies are common in the northern parts of the country in the summer. They may be found wherever milkweeds grow. Their eggs are laid on these plants, and the pretty black and white and yellow caterpillars eat the leaves. These striped caterpillars change to green *chrysalises*. Later the chrysalis cases are torn open by the grown butterflies that come out of them.

After they come out of the chrysalis cases, the monarchs go from flower to flower and feast on the nectar they find. After a while, however, they gather in flocks and fly to the South. Their wings are buff and black on the under side and rich reddish brown and black on the upper side. The flocks of these flying insects look like enormous clouds when they pass overhead. They rest during the night on convenient trees. Then the trees look as if they had beautiful buff and tawny leaves.

We call animals *migrants* if they travel, or migrate, from one region to another.

Some kinds of fish spend the summer and winter in the same or neighboring places. But many kinds of fish have times of migrating. In another chapter you read about salmon that migrate from salt water to spend their spawning season in fresh water.

Eels leave their fresh-water homes and go into salt water before they lay their eggs. Great numbers of these fish travel together. They take an interesting journey.

After they leave the lakes and rivers where they have been living, they travel far, far away. At last they reach the deep waters that lie to the south of Bermuda. This is the place where they spawn. One mother eel may have as many as five or ten million eggs. So all the mother eels that go south to that spawning place must deposit millions and billions of eggs.

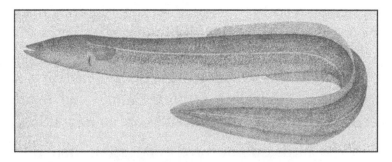

This eel is twenty-five inches long.

Chickadees and woodpeckers and some other birds stay in one region all through the year. But many kinds of birds are migrants that travel northward in the spring until they come to their nesting places. In the fall they go south, where it is easy for them to find food.

Bobolinks are such migrants. They go so far south, indeed, that they cannot wait for the leaves to turn yellow and red before they start. Some flocks begin their journey the very last of July. Others follow at different times during August.

The birds of course do not need to buy tickets or maps or compasses before they go. But they do get ready for their journey in some ways. They have new suits of feathers. The fall traveling coats of the bobolinks are nearly alike. The fathers and sons look almost like the mothers and daughters. All are dressed in dull buff, streaked and spotted with dark brown and black.

The father bobolinks seem to forget their marvelous spring songs when they lose their showy black and white and yellow feathers. They do not have much to say except "Chink." "Chink," indeed, is the bobolinks' fall signal—a sort of password for the migrating flock. They need a signal, for they fly by night as well as by day. So they call to one another, and each bird can tell when it is near the others. Sometimes people, listening at night, hear voices calling, "Chink! Chink!" high in the air. Then they know the bobolinks are going south.

These birds do not travel very fast at first. They need fuel for their journey. They do not get gasoline for engines of course, but they must have fat in their bodies. The oily fat is a sort of fuel for them.

Bobolinks catch a great many insects during their stay in the North. They feed their nestlings with grasshoppers and other meadow insects. They help the grass crop in this way and save a great deal of hay for northern farmers. The young bobolinks must have insects to eat. This meat food is good for their growth.

But while the flocks are going southward, they find delicious grains that are soft and milky. They stop for picnics now and then. Wild rice, growing in marshes in New Jersey, Maryland, Virginia, and other places, is a favorite food of the bobolinks. It is starchy and they become fat as they eat it. They like cultivated rice, too. In the South these birds are called rice-birds.

The bobolinks' journey

The flocks that pass through South Carolina go south to Florida. But they do not stop there. Their travels are not yet half over. They fly across the water to Cuba and rest there for a while. From Cuba the migrants fly to Central or South America. Many of them, however, stop in Jamaica and spend some time there in October. They are known as butter-birds on that island, because they are so very fat.

There is no place for them to rest during the long flight from Jamaica to the coast of Central or South America. They must fly at least four hundred miles across the water. People think they take this long flight in a single night. But they are not too tired to go on and on. They fly over great forests. They go across the Amazon River. At last they reach marshy places along the Paraguay River; there they have their winter homes.

The fields in northern United States are not without flocks of birds in winter even though all the birds that nest there have gone south. Snow buntings, or "snowflakes," as they are also called, fly from arctic lands to this part of the country to spend their winter.

These migrants do not mind the weather they find in the northern part of our country. They run on the hard snowy crust without freezing their feet. They wade through soft snow, leaving little trails behind them. On sunny days they take snow baths as cheerfully as hens take dust baths in hot summer weather.

Snow buntings need migrate only far enough to find fields where the snow is not too deep to cover the seedy tops of meadow plants. In such places they twitter happily while they feast on the seeds.

Before the snow is quite gone from these fields they start back to their northern homes. There in warm, sunny spots, during the arctic summer, they make their nests—lining them, oftentimes, with hair shed from the coats of reindeer.

What To Do after Reading Chapter Five

TRAVELING WITH BOBOLINKS

Suppose that you could follow a flock of migrating bobolinks. You might start with some of these birds that had spent the summer in the most northern state on the eastern coast (Maine) and go with them to a marshy place near the Paraguay River in South America.

Make a list of some of the places where they might stop for food and rest.

Look on a globe or other maps for all the places you have in your list.

TRAVELING WITH EELS

Suppose that you could travel with some eels that migrated from a river in northeastern United States. Look on a globe or other maps to see where you would go before you could find a place in the Atlantic Ocean south of the Bermuda Islands.

THE MIGRANTS

I may not go to tropic lands,
　　Where summer comes in winter time,
To seek what birds, sojourning there,
　　Make holiday in sunny clime.

And yet they are not strange to me—
 Those prairie birds of Paraguay.
I hear their jubilating tones.
 I recognize their fair array.

For tropic zones cannot retain
 The joy of _____ in spring.
That they may camp on northern meads,
 They hither haste with eager wing.

Copy these twelve lines of verse and put the right name of migrating birds in the tenth line. Ask your teacher the meaning of any word in these lines you do not understand. Then write the same thoughts in prose form.

READ

Read one or more of the following selections:

(1) "Bob, the Vagabond," the last chapter in *Bird Stories*.

(2) "A Creature of Mystery—the Eel," pages 22–24 in *Nature Narratives*, Volume I.

(3) "Migratory Butterflies," pages 55–57 in *Nature Narratives*, Volume I.

(4) "Snowflakes," a chapter in *Holiday Meadow*.

CHAPTER VI

RIPE LEAVES

Strawberries are green while they are small, before they begin to ripen. So are apples and plums and, indeed, most of our fruits. It is only when fruits are ripe and ready to be eaten that their rich and inviting colors are most beautiful.

We may speak of ripe leaves as well as of ripe fruit. Leaves are ripe when they have lost their green color and have become yellow or red.

You cannot pick a green strawberry without breaking the stem. The fruit is held tightly in place while it is growing. But the plant lets its ripe fruit fall. You can pull off a perfectly ripe berry without tearing any of the green part of the plant. Some fruits, like holly berries and rose hips and Japanese barberries, stay on the branches for months after they are ripe. But most juicy ripe fruits of trees and bushes fall from the branches that held them fast while they were growing.

Ripe leaves drop as easily and naturally as such ripe fruits. A breath of wind is strong enough to pick them from the branches, when the right time comes.

Raking up the fallen leaves

What happens to a leaf to change it so that it can fall without being torn? A weak place is formed at the base of its stem just where it joins the branch. Rows of tiny cells grow across this place. There they change to a thin, corky layer. The leaf loses its hold on the twig as the corky layer dries. At last it falls.

The corky spot from which the leaf dropped is now like a little scar. There is no moist injury on the twig. Instead, there is a dry, healthy scar as if a slight wound had already been healed.

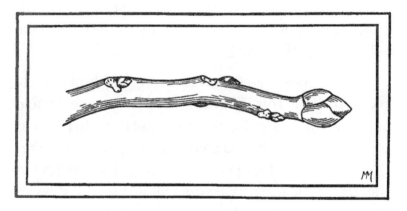

Notice the scars on the branch.

All summer the healthy leaves of most trees are green. They are green because there are little particles in them that have a green color. These particles keep their green color for a while and then lose it. They become colorless. The particles do this all summer. But the leaves themselves remain green because the tree keeps making more and more of these tiny particles every day.

In the fall, however, a tree that is to lose its leaves

stops making any more of this green material. When the old green particles become colorless, there are none to take their places. So the leaves themselves are no longer green.

Most leaves are yellow after the green color fades from them. This is because there are yellow particles in the leaves. The yellow particles are there all summer; but they do not show then, for the yellow color is hidden by the green color. The healthy summer leaves may be yellowish green, but they cannot be clear golden yellow. After the green color disappears, the pure yellow can show. Elms and lindens and many other trees have yellow leaves in the fall.

Some kinds of green leaves become partly or entirely red in the fall. This is because they have considerable sugar and other substances that cause them to turn red in the sunshine. The red color forms in the leaves after the green color disappears. Red leaves have yellow in them, too. The reason why the yellow does not show in the red places is that the red color hides the yellow.

Some maple trees have leaves that may turn either red or yellow. The red color comes in the leaves that are where most light can reach them. The yellow leaves are those growing in the more shaded places. If one maple leaf covers another, the upper leaf may be red but the lower, shaded leaf will be yellow.

It is quite interesting to learn that green leaves have yellow in them all summer, and that red autumn leaves have yellow in them, too. We could not tell, just by looking at the leaves, that there is yellow hidden by the green or red.

What To Do after Reading Chapter Six

TAKE GREEN COLOR FROM LEAVES

Put a few soft, thin green leaves into a test tube or other glass dish that hot water will not break. Cover the leaves with alcohol[1] and water (about four fifths alcohol and one fifth water). Lower the test tube into a dish of hot water. Watch the alcohol become green. The green color comes out of the leaves.

TAKE YELLOW COLOR FROM LEAVES

Put several yellow leaves into a test tube. Cover the leaves with alcohol[1] and water (about four fifths alcohol). Lower the test tube into a dish of hot water. Watch the alcohol become yellow. Take the leaves out of the alcohol. Are they still yellow?

TAKE RED COLOR FROM LEAVES

Put a number of very bright red leaves into a test tube. Cover the leaves with water only. Lower the test

[1]Do not have the alcohol near any flame. It would be better to boil the water in one room and use the alcohol in another. If you keep the alcohol away from flame, there is no danger in doing these experiments.

tube into a dish of hot water. Watch the water in the test tube become red. Remove the leaves from the test tube. What color are they now?

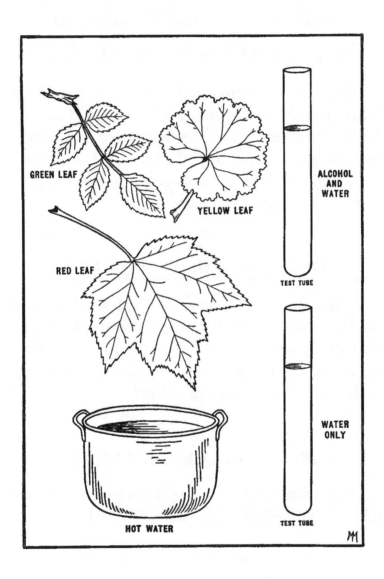

CHAPTER VII

HARVESTING FOOD
FOR WINTER

Animals living in most southern parts of our country do not need to prepare for cold weather. Although they find the winter season different from the summer time, they do not meet ice or snow.

But there is ice on rivers and lakes in most northern parts of the United States in winter, and there is snow on the ground. Animals staying in these places must be ready for cold weather. Some sleep. Some hunt. Some store food.

Men harvest food and store it for use in winter. Potatoes, beets, carrots, apples, and some other foods keep well in cellars that are cool and not too dry.

Squirrels, too, harvest food to eat in winter. Much of it they store in hollows in old trees or in the ground. Some of it they put into holes which they dig for cellars. You may have watched a squirrel bury an acorn. Perhaps you noticed him when he ran across the grass with one of these nuts in his mouth. Then he stopped and dug a hole with his front paws. He moved them so rapidly

The seeds are still inside these cones.

you could hardly see what he was doing. In a moment he tucked his acorn into the hole. He patted the ground over it before he went frisking off for another acorn.

Gray squirrels harvest the big cones of pines and Norway spruces. They do this late in the summer while the cones are still closed and a little green. Then the seeds are inside the cones. If a squirrel waited until the cones were brown and ripe and open, the seeds would be scattered on the ground. It is not much work for him to cut off a cone and let it drop with all its seeds inside. But it would take him much longer to pick up all those seeds after they had fallen from the cone.

The squirrel scampers from branch tip to branch tip, hunting for cones. His teeth are so sharp that he can cut a cone with one quick snip. In a few minutes all the cones that were on the tree will be scattered about the ground. Then he picks them up and places them in a big heap near the base of the tree. Later the weather will be cold and the heap will be covered with snow. But the squirrel will not mind. He can dig a tunnel through the snow. His food is ready for winter.

The red squirrel, Chickaree, likes the seeds of arbor-vitae cones. *Arbor vitae* is a pleasant name; it means *tree of life*. Arbor-vitae cones grow in clusters. Chickaree does not cut one small cone at a time. He nips the tip of a twig, and the whole cluster falls. Each cluster has many cones and each cone has ten or more seeds.

Chickaree begins his harvest about the first of September. The cones are not ripe then. They are still almost cream colored and have a tint of pale green.

Their scales are tightly closed and the seeds are safe inside. Harvesting arbor-vitae cones seems to be a merry game for Chickaree. He jumps and climbs from branch to branch of these evergreen trees. And all the while the cut cone clusters drop with little sliding and thumping sounds as they hit the lower branches and the ground.

Chickaree cut this cluster of cones.

The small red squirrel is cheerful as long as no one comes into his hunting ground. But if he should see you watching him, he would bark at you. His bark sounds like a cough, a sneeze, a growl, and a squeal—all mixed together. It would make you laugh.

Chickaree uses cold storage for his unripe cones. He digs holes in cool, damp moss and stores some of his clusters there. But he piles most of them in shady hollows. In some of his biggest cellars he has hundreds of clusters with thousands of cones. So Chickaree is ready for cold weather, too.

People who live in the North put storm doors outside their other doors for winter. They have storm windows, too, to cover their other windows. Sometimes they bank their houses near the ground with sloping "banking" boards or straw or evergreen boughs. They do what they can to keep the cold air outside and the warmth inside their homes.

Ondatra, the muskrat, prepares his house for winter. He builds his thick walls so snug that winter air cannot get through. He banks his home with no one to show him how.

The winter home of Ondatra, the muskrat

Muskrats do not need thick-walled shelter in the summer. They dig caves in the banks of meadow streams. Or they camp in dry tussocks, or tufts, they find in marshes. Old clumps of tough, round rush stems and their long leaves make good summer homes for them. Bunches of three-cornered sedge stems do quite as well.

In the fall, however, the muskrats begin to build for winter. Several of them work together. They build busily in the evening and very early in the morning and while the moon is bright. They make heaps with dry sedge and rush stems and leaves. They pile muddy roots on the outside, and the mud helps plaster the walls. Inside the heap, they dig a room where they can rest and keep warm. Their doors lead down cellar into the water, where they store roots for food. Then the muskrats are ready for cold weather—with a warm home and cold-storage food.

What To Do after Reading Chapter Seven

READ

Read "The Cone Hunt," a chapter in *Holiday Hill*.

Read "A Beaver's House," in Chapter 14 in *First Lessons in Nature Study*.

WRITE

Choose one of the following subjects and write about it. Write fifty words or more.

(1) Chickaree Hunts for Seeds.

(2) Some Beavers Build a House.

(3) Some Muskrats Make a Winter Home.

BUILD

Build a room shaped like a muskrat's winter home. Use dry grass stems or grasslike plants for the walls. Plaster the walls on the outside with something to make them firm. Use mud if you wish. Use some other kind of plaster if you prefer. If you use a light plaster, you might color it dark to make it look like mud.

CHAPTER VIII

WHITE CRYSTALS

There are many boys and girls who have never played with snowballs and who have never made a snow man. There are many who have never seen even one flake of snow. Other boys and girls, who live far away in Arctic places, are much better acquainted with snow than with green leaves.

But most of those who read this book are living where it is not too warm for at least some snow in winter. Yet they can see bare or grassy ground much longer each year than they can look at snow.

One dainty little snowflake seems too frail to amount to much in the world. Yet each flake is important. A flake that falls on some distant mountain top may help other flakes there to form a mighty *glacier*, or moving bed of ice. Some mountain tops are so cold that the snow there does not melt and run off in rapid brooks. Instead, the snow that is underneath becomes packed by the heavy weight of the countless millions of snow particles on top of it. After years and years, the snow is pressed so hard that it becomes a firm mass of ice.

Such a mass of ice, or glacier, moves slowly down

the mountain side, grinding and crushing as it goes. If this river of ice reaches the sea, parts of it break off and become *icebergs*. Some glaciers reach lakes and melt there.

Icebergs break from glaciers.

Glaciers cover some of the peaks of the Rocky Mountains. There are beautiful lakes in the valleys of Glacier National Park in Montana. The water in them is from melting glaciers that form on the mountains far above.

Most of the snow, however, that falls in the United States does not settle on mountains. It covers forests and fields. It reaches cities and country places.

On city streets and sidewalks, snow is a nuisance; it must be cleared away. Snow on many country roads, too, must be pushed out of the way by giant snowplows, so that automobiles may travel there. Heavy snows always mean work to be done so that traffic may continue.

Snow means pleasure as well as work. Boys and girls like to build snow huts and make statues of snow shaped like animals and people. Children, and grown persons too, like to coast down slopes on sleds and toboggans. They enjoy snowshoe hikes in places where they cannot walk with ordinary shoes.

Snowflakes are useful in many ways. They collect on mountains and in woods, where they melt slowly in the spring. In this way they give a gradual supply of water, which might otherwise rush away and be lost before it could be used. The water supply of some cities comes from snow that gathers on far-away mountains in winter and melts in spring and summer.

Snow keeps the ground moist for northern trees and other plants in winter. Of course such plants do not need so much water while they are resting in winter as they do while they are growing in summer. But even a winter drought does great damage to plant life. A blanket of snow on the ground prevents the moisture in the earth from *evaporating*, or going off in the form of vapor.

A blanket of snow also prevents the ground from becoming warmer or colder. Many plants that usually live through the winter would die if the ground should freeze too deeply. Or plants might start to grow if the ground thawed on mild, sunny winter days. Then they would die during colder weather. The snow blanket, however, keeps the temperature of the ground even. The

A snow blanket keeps the temperature of the ground even.

reason it can do this is that there are countless little air pockets among the snowflakes. These air pockets keep the heat and the cold from passing through.

No dust can blow from ground that is covered with snow. The air at such a place is clean. We say that such clean, cool air is bracing. It is very pleasant to breathe.

What are the dainty little snowflakes that, taken together, amount to so much in the world? Of course you know that they are bits of frozen water. Perhaps you would like to know that they are often called *crystals*.

Certain substances take shapes in regular patterns when they change from a liquid state to a solid. Each regularly shaped bit of such a substance is called a crystal. There are salt crystals, sugar crystals, diamond crystals, and crystals of many other substances. But there are no crystals in the world that are more beautiful than water crystals, or snowflakes. You may be interested to catch some flakes on a piece of black cloth some day when it is snowing. Their shapes show well on black.

A man who lived in Vermont studied many thousands of snowflakes. He said he never saw two snowflakes that were just alike. Of course he could not remember all the thousands of shapes unless he had pictures of them. And, in fact, he was so much interested in snowflakes that he took their photographs.

This man worked in a room that was not heated. The snowflakes fell through a hole made for them in the roof. He caught them on black velvet. He wished to have pictures that were larger than the flakes so that their patterns could easily be seen. For that purpose he used a camera attached to a microscope. Many of his snowflake pictures have been printed in books.

What To Do after Reading Chapter Eight

SALT CRYSTALS

Get a little salt from a salt bag and look at the crystals. Look through a magnifying glass if there is one you can use. Are they shaped like any snow crystals (or pictures of snow crystals) you have ever seen? If not, what differences do you find?

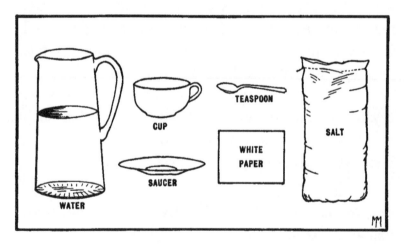

Would you like to look at some newly formed salt crystals? Then follow these directions:

(1) Put 5 spoonfuls of cold or hot water into a cup.

(2) Put 2 spoonfuls of salt (or a little more if the water you use is warm or hot) into the cup with the water.

(3) Stir the salt in the water until *most* of it has dissolved. (If it *all* dissolves, add a little more salt.)

(4) Place a slip of clean white paper in a saucer.

(5) Pour the clear salty water from the cup into the saucer so that it covers the paper. (Do not pour out any of the salt in the bottom of the cup.)

(6) Leave the saucer in a quiet place until the water has gone off in vapor. The salt that was dissolved in the water will not go away with the vapor. It will be left in the saucer, in the form of crystals. Look at the crystals that you find resting on the paper.

Some of the class may leave saucers in cold places, and some may leave them in warm places. The crystals will form more slowly in the cold places, but they will be larger. Have the small salt crystals and the large salt crystals the same shape? Do they look like snow crystals?

SUGAR CRYSTALS

Dissolve all the sugar you can in 5 spoonfuls of hot or cold water. Notice whether you can dissolve more than 2 spoonfuls. Pour the clear sugary water into a dish in which you have a slip of paper or a piece of white string. After the water has gone off as vapor, do you find sugar crystals resting on the paper or string? If so, are they shaped like salt crystals?

SNOW CRYSTALS

Earlier you read of a man in Vermont who photographed and studied snowflakes. If you wish to know his name, look under the snowflake pictures in "Water" in *Surprises*.

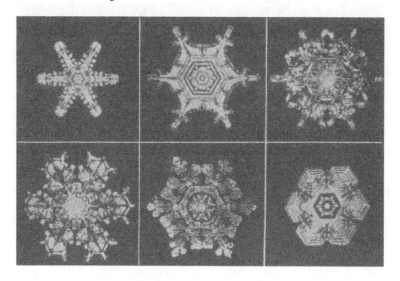

Notice the shapes of these snowflakes.

There are pictures of six snowflakes on that page and pictures of six others on this page. Although no two of these flakes have exactly the same shape, they are all alike in one way. They all have six sides and six corners.

Find the word *snow* in a dictionary. Look for pictures of snow crystals near this word. Count the outer corners of each crystal. How many are there?

Find the word *hexagon* in a dictionary. Is there

a six-cornered picture near this word? You may be interested to know that *hex* is a Greek word meaning *six* and *gonia* (*gon*) is a Greek word meaning *corner*.

Copy, as well as you can, a picture of a snowflake on a piece of paper. Then draw straight lines connecting the outer corners. Have you a hexagon around your snowflake picture?

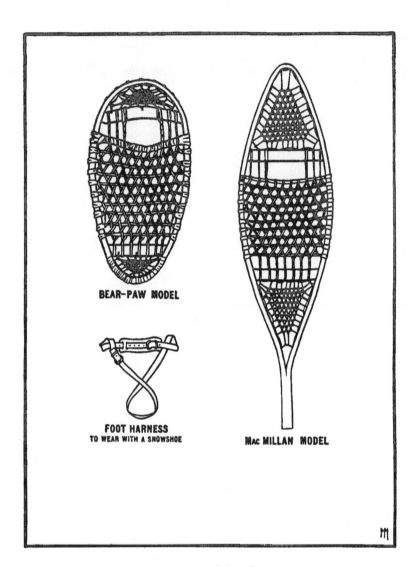

Snowshoes and foot harness

CHAPTER IX

SNOWSHOES

It is easy for you to walk or run on firm ground. Good stout shoes are suitable to wear for tramps over fields, up hillsides, or through woods when the ground is hard enough.

When you come to a boggy place, however, your feet may sink into the mud. It is hard to walk there. Perhaps it is dangerous, too, for you may need some one to pull you out. If you think of ducks and geese at such a time, you will realize how fortunate they are to have broad, flat feet, for they can stay on top of the mud and not sink as you do.

It is as pleasant to walk or run on firm snow as on dry ground, unless there happens to be an icy, slippery crust on top. But if you try to walk on soft snow, your feet go down much as they do in mud. You flounder in a helpless way and soon become very tired. Ordinary boots or shoes are not suitable to wear for a long walk on soft snow. You need something broad and flat on your feet.

A broad snowshoe has a curved outer frame of strong wood. Strips of strong hide are woven from side to side and from front to back on this frame. Eskimos and Indians living in North America have long used broad-webbed snowshoes of different patterns. They have taught white people how to make them. Such shoes are the best kind to wear when walking on soft snow.

Climbing a hill on skis

A ski is another sort of snowshoe. It is a long narrow runner with its front tip turned up in a curve. Skis have been used for many years in Norway and certain other parts of Europe. They have been introduced into North America. People can go much faster on skis than on broad snowshoes if the surface of the snow is firm or crusted with ice. A pair of skis, too, serve like the runners of a sled for sliding rapidly down hills. It is fun to use them in winter sports.

Some birds wear snowshoes in winter. Their snowshoes grow on their feet in the fall and come off in the spring, when they are no longer needed.

The ruffed grouse (often called partridges) are birds whose feet change with the seasons. In winter there are horny fringes on their toes that make their feet broader. It is easy for them to walk on snow. Their feet are without such fringes in summer.

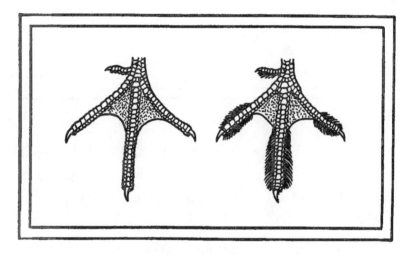

Foot of grouse in summer (left) and in winter (right)

These birds do not migrate to warm countries in winter. They are hardy and can take care of themselves in cold weather. During pleasant days they often feast on birch seeds scattered on the snow. They find berries that still cling to branches in winter. And they like the taste of winter buds of certain trees and bushes. At night and during stormy days they rest in cozy little caves they dig in the snow.

Some kinds of furry animals wear snowshoes in winter. The varying hare has large hind feet with long toes. In winter these toes are covered with very thick hair that forms a broad pad on each hind foot. That is why he is also called the snowshoe rabbit.

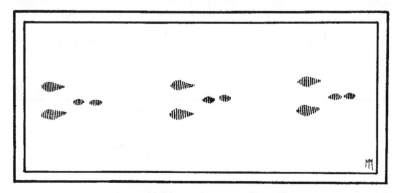

Tracks of the snowshoe rabbit

It is fun for boys and girls to wade in deep, fresh snow for a little while. They like to roll and play in it. But they are glad to put on snowshoes if they go for a real hike.

If you were to visit certain parts of Alaska, you might see horses traveling over deep snow on snowshoes. Men there often help their horses by fastening snowshoes to their feet. You may understand why these animals need such help if you will notice the shape of a horse's hoofs.

Jack would need snowshoes if he were going far.

What To Do after Reading Chapter Nine

WHY DO SNOWSHOES HELP?

Fill a small box with snow or fine sand or flour or other powdery stuff.

Press a toy foot (a doll's foot will do) into this. Does it go down far and easily?

Make a toy snowshoe and fasten it to the foot. Press this into the snow (or other powdery stuff). Does it go down as easily and as far as it did before?

Why do snowshoes help one to walk on snow?

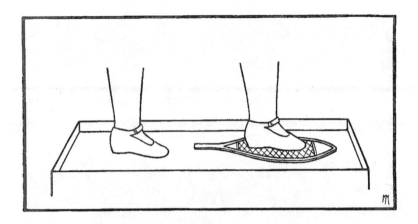

READ

Read "Little Snowshoes," a chapter in *Holiday Hill.*

CHAPTER X

DORMANT ANIMALS

Dorm is part of a Latin word meaning *sleep*. It helps to form some English words that have to do with sleeping. Thus a *dormitory* is a place where people sleep. And *dormant* means *sleeping* or *resting*.

All birds that stay in the North are active in winter. They must find plenty of food or they cannot live. They may starve if the snow is too deep or the trees and bushes are covered with sleet. That is why thoughtful people put seeds on the crusty snow for seed-eating birds and fasten suet to trees for birds that need meat.

Some furry animals are active during the winter months even in the northern parts of the United States. Chickaree, the red squirrel, fills his pantries and cellars with good food in the fall and has plenty for his winter feasts. Little Snowshoes, the varying hare, hops across the snow and nibbles the bark of birch and poplar trees when he is hungry for his picnic dinner. There is food for both of them even when the ground is covered with deep snow.

There are other furry animals, or mammals, however, that do not gather a harvest of food for winter use, as

Chickaree does. Neither can they find what they need to eat, as does the varying hare, or snowshoe rabbit. Such animals have a strange way of passing through the coldest weather. They neither eat nor starve. They remain dormant, day and night, in a wonderful sleep that lasts for weeks or even months.

Bats, bears, chipmunks, jumping mice, raccoons, skunks, and woodchucks are seven kinds of animals that can doze through the cold season without eating anything.

To be sure, these animals are not entirely without food all this time even though they do not eat. They are fat, from eating a great deal in the fall, before they become dormant. Their sleeping bodies can make use of this fat as a sort of food to keep them alive. Perhaps, at the same time, the fat itself helps make them feel sleepy.

It is quite likely, too, that the bad air in their winter rooms helps keep them asleep, for most of them rest in close dens or caves. You may have noticed how stupid and drowsy you feel if you stay in a room where the air is not fresh. Animals cannot be very wide awake if they do not have plenty of *oxygen* to breathe. There is not much of this healthful gas in the air of snug winter dens. And every time a dormant animal breathes he uses up a little more of the oxygen.

Such an animal, however, does not breathe very often or very deeply. He may, indeed, breathe only one hundredth as often as he would breathe when awake or when having an ordinary short sleep in summer. So he

The woodchuck has been dormant in his den,
but he is awake now and on his way out.

really gets along with very little oxygen.

His heart beats very slowly, too. If you should feel his pulse, you might not notice any motion at all—it is so slow and feeble. For the rate of his heartbeats may be only about one eightieth as fast as during a night's sleep in summer.

The body of the dormant animal has nothing but its own fat to nourish it. He breathes only a little air, and that air is likely not to be pure. So only a small amount of oxygen reaches the blood. Of course a body that does not have a usual sort of food and a usual amount of oxygen must be in an unusual condition in many ways. One important difference is in its blood. The blood has less sugar in it than it has at other times of the year, when the animal is awake and eating.

Something very special, then, happens to a really dormant animal. His blood grows cool. The blood of a woodchuck in his winter quarters is only a little warmer than the air in his den. If you should put a thermometer into his mouth, you would find that his temperature is much lower than it is in the spring or summer or fall.

Only certain warm-blooded animals can live if their blood changes more than a few degrees. If you put a thermometer into your own mouth in winter, you will find that your temperature is the same as in summer. It will be about 98 degrees if you are well. If you have a fever, the thermometer will register a few degrees higher than 98. It may drop a few degrees lower than 98 under some conditions. But in all your life your blood cannot change more than a few degrees either higher or lower.

The body temperature of some dormant mammals, however, may sink until it is about 30 degrees lower than it is at other seasons of the year. It is very remarkable that certain warm-blooded animals can live through such a change of body temperature when most of them cannot.

All dormant mammals do not sleep with equal soundness. A bear is one of the lighter sleepers. A woodchuck is one of the soundest sleepers of them all. He cannot see the brightest light. He cannot hear the loudest noise. He cannot feel anything that may touch his body.

It does not seem quite so strange that cold-blooded animals can lie dormant during a northern winter, for their body temperatures change at all times of the year with the temperatures of the places where they happen to be. Their blood is warm if they are resting on a warm rock in the bright sunshine of a summer day. Their blood is cold, even in summer, if they are in cold water or in a cool, shady cave.

Lizards, snakes, turtles, toads, and frogs are some of the cold-blooded animals with backbones. All such animals that dwell in the North are dormant during the coldest part of the year.

Cold-blooded animals without backbones are dormant in winter, too, if they live in the North.

A dormant snake

Earthworms go into their deepest tunnels and lie together in tangled bunches. Snails seek sheltered places and close the openings in their shells with layers of lime. Each kind of animal has its own way of facing a season during which it cannot eat.

Among the six-footed animals, or insects, there are different ways of passing a northern winter.

The yellow-edge butterfly and certain other butterflies go into hollows in old trees and rest there while the weather is cold. They pass the winter as full-grown insects, or *adults*.

The swallowtail butterflies, which change from caterpillars to *chrysalids* (or chrysalises) in the late summer or fall, remain in this condition until spring. Then they break the chrysalid cases and fly away.

Another kind of butterfly, called the Baltimore, does

not change to a chrysalid before winter. A whole brood of Baltimore caterpillars live in a tent they make by weaving leaves together with silk. In this tent they spend the winter. And, strange as it may seem, they refrain from eating, also, during the late summer and fall. They fast, indeed, for about nine months. Then, when the leaves on their food plant are fresh and tender in the spring, they begin to eat and complete their growth.

A young queen bumblebee sleeps in some good little den until spring.

Many moths live as *pupae* (in cocoons) during the winter. Some live in the caterpillar stage. Some spend the winter in the egg stage.

Some crickets do not hatch from eggs until spring. Some pass the winter as young wingless crickets in small caves.

An insect has four different stages in its life: (1) egg; (2) larva (such as caterpillar, grub, or maggot); (3) pupa (called chrysalis if the insect is a butterfly); (4) adult. Certain insects pass the winter as eggs, others as larvae, others as pupae, and still others as adults.

What To Do after Reading Chapter Ten

RIDDLES

My blood is hardly warmer than the air.
I sleep the winter through without a care.
And when I waken it is early spring—
Quite time for me to jump and swim and sing.
What am I?

I pass, in silent sleep, the winter days.
Ere summer comes I wake and change my ways.
I visit, one by one, the flowers of June
On wings that whir a happy humming tune.
What am I?

NAME TWO OR MORE

Name two or more warm-blooded furry animals that are dormant in winter. Name two or more that are active in winter.

Name two or more warm-blooded feathered animals that are active in winter. Did you ever hear of one that is dormant?

Name two or more cold-blooded animals, with backbones, that are dormant in winter. Do you know of any that are active in very cold winter weather?

READ

Read "One Kind of Gas," in the Air chapter in *Surprises*.

Each of the following selections tells about some creature that is dormant in winter. Choose one or more to read.

(1) "The Yelping Frog," a chapter in *Holiday Pond*.

(2) "Lotor, the Washer," a chapter in *Holiday Pond*.

(3) "Whistling Wejack," a chapter in *Holiday Meadow*.

(4) "Van, the Sleepy Butterfly," a chapter in *Hexapod Stories*.

(5) "Old Bumble," a chapter in *Hexapod Stories*.

WRITE

Write a story about some animal that is dormant in winter and active in summer. You may choose any dormant animal that is mentioned in this chapter. Tell what it does in summer. Tell what sort of place it uses for its winter dormitory.

If you like to write with rhymes, write a verse about some dormant animal.

If you think it would be fun, write a riddle about one of these animals.

This old willow shed its leaves and rested all winter.

CHAPTER XI

DORMANT PLANTS

What are plants doing when winter comes? Are they dormant, too, while the woodchuck is stiff and still and senseless in his den?

Yes, northern plants must rest during the cold months if they are to keep well and strong. Sometimes trees and bushes start to grow during a midwinter thaw. But this is very serious for them, because the tender leaves are killed as soon as there is freezing weather again. Days and nights that are steadily cold are much better for plants in winter. It is best for them not to grow until the spring weather is so mild that the new leaves and flowers can live.

Plants have different ways of spending the winter.

Most of the broad-leaf trees and bushes and climbing vines shed their old leaves in fall. The beginnings, or winter buds, of new leaves and flowers are on the twigs during the cold months; but they do not open and grow until spring. They are protected by tough scales.

These scales are covered with varnish. This substance prevents the moisture inside the buds from escaping.

It keeps them from becoming too dry. It also prevents the water from melting snow or sleet from soaking into the buds and later freezing there.

The varnish on the overwintering buds of the balsam poplar tree is a fragrant resin or gum. People like the odor of this and sometimes add it to ointments.

Some broad-leaf trees and bushes, like the holly tree and laurel bushes, keep their old green leaves all winter. They are called evergreen plants. The leaves of such plants are tough and can stand freezing weather. Even these evergreen plants, however, hold their new growth safely tucked inside their small winter buds until spring, when they begin to unfold as leaves and blossoms.

Balsam poplar twigs with winter buds

Most of the vines that retain their old leaves in winter grow close to the ground. There are a number of northern evergreen vines that creep in woody places. One of these is called the partridge berry because the ruffed grouse (often called a partridge, you remember) is very glad to have a midwinter feast of the bright red berries that grow on this vine.

Partridge and partridge berries

Cone-bearing trees do not have broad leaves. The tamarack is a cone-bearing tree that sheds its leaves every fall. All our other cone-bearing trees are evergreens. It is only their old leaves that show on the evergreens during the winter, however. The flowers and new leaves do not come out until spring.

Underground parts of many kinds of plants can live after the upper parts have been killed by the frost.

The tamarack has cones, but it is not an evergreen.

The stems and leaves of potato plants die down to the ground when freezing weather comes. In many places potatoes, if left in the ground, can live and grow in the spring. But, as you know, this is not the way that potatoes are grown in fields for the market.

Many plants of the Lily Family and some other families have underground bulbs. A bulb is really a special thickened kind of leaf bud. Such a bud lives through the winter. The leafy parts of the plant grow from the bulb in the spring.

Some of the earliest spring flowers we have in our gardens come from bulbs. The purple crocus grows wild in meadows in some parts of Europe. People often plant crocus bulbs in their lawns in this country. Then in the spring the plants grow as if they were at home in a meadow.

People plant the bulbs of snowdrops about their homes in this country, too. Snowdrops grow wild in woods and shady pastures in Europe. The slender little plants look very frail indeed. Yet the stems can push their way through thin, crusty ice and show their dainty, nodding blossoms before the snow is gone in spring.

Snowdrops

Plants scatter their seeds when they are ripe. Many kinds of seeds lie on the ground until the next spring before they sprout.

Some plants make their whole growth in a single summer. The scarlet field poppy needs but a few months in which to grow from the seed and have seeds of its own to scatter before winter comes.

The mullein and evening primrose and many other

plants do not have blossoms until their second summer. Only a flat cluster of leaves grows the first summer. These leaves spread like a round mat on the ground and live all winter. Such a cluster is called an overwintering *rosette*. A tall stem grows from the center of the rosette in the spring. This stem bears leaves and blossoms.

Overwintering rosette of evening primrose

What To Do after Reading Chapter Eleven

LOOKING FOR WINTER ROSETTES

The word *rosette* is used in several different ways. In one way, as you have learned, it is used to mean a cluster of leaves arranged in circles.

Take a winter walk while there is little or no snow on the ground. Walk in the country or in a city park or in a school garden. Look for plants that pass the winter in the form of rosettes. See how many different kinds you can find.

Remember your outdoor good manners and do not disturb any rosette that should not be touched. However, some of our most common and troublesome weeds have overwintering rosettes. Perhaps you or your teacher can find a dandelion rosette or one of some other common weed that may be brought to school.

If you have a rosette at school, draw a picture of it. See if you can draw a rosette design that would make a pretty border for a winter plant chart.

LOOKING AT WINTER TWIGS

Take a winter walk in the country or in a park where trees and bushes may be found.

Do you find any evergreens? Are there any evergreens with broad leaves among the trees and bushes you find in your walk?

Look at bare twigs. The winter buds on one kind of tree or bush are not just like those on any other kind. Learn to notice differences in size, shape, and position of the winter buds on leafless twigs.

If you see anyone pruning branches from his trees or bushes in the winter, ask for some of the twigs. Use samples of them on your winter plant chart.

A SEED HUNT

See how many different kinds of seeds you can find on plants out of doors in winter. Look at them through a magnifying glass. Make pictures of them for your winter plant chart. Make the pictures much larger than the seeds.

A LUNCHEON FOR SNOW BUNTINGS

In a previous chapter you read about some birds that migrate from arctic regions to our northern states to spend the winter. While you are having the seed hunt mentioned on the previous page, notice how high different plants hold their seeds. About how deep would the snow need to be to hide the tops of clover stems so that these birds could not find clover seeds to eat? Could the birds find goldenrod seeds if the snow were a foot deep? If you do not find clover and goldenrod seeds, notice how high above the ground some other kinds of seeds are.

Write a short composition about a luncheon of seeds for snow buntings.

WINTER PLANT CHART

Prepare a good chart to show how some plants look in winter. Have samples of plants. You should also have the drawings of plants that have been suggested on this page and the previous page.

ANNUALS AND OTHER PLANTS

We hear some plants spoken of as annuals. (The name *annual* comes from a Latin word meaning *year*.) Annuals blossom in the same year in which they are raised from seeds. Their roots do not live over winter. They are one-year plants.

Some plants are called *biennials*. (*Bi* means *two*.) Biennials do not blossom the same year in which they are raised from seeds but wait until the second year. Their roots live over one winter.

Plants whose roots live through many years are called *perennials*. (*Per* means *through*.)

Look in a plant catalogue to find the names of some annuals and some perennials.

Stand with your back to the sun to see rainbow colors.

CHAPTER XII

SHORT LIGHT WAVES

Sunshine is more dazzling to the eyes when snow is on the ground than when the earth is green with leafy plants. This is because the white snow reflects the sunlight. The sunlight itself is not really brighter in winter than it is in summer. It is not, indeed, so bright in the northern half of the world.

When we look at the air in the daytime, the light seems colorless to us. We say that sunlight is white. This white light really has different colors in it. None of them shows while they are mixed together. But there are ways of breaking sunlight into different colors that we can see.

We see colors in a rainbow. That is because sunlight touches the raindrops or mist in the air. At such times the white light is broken into colors, which are reflected by the drops of water. The colors you can see in the rainbow are red, orange, yellow, green, blue, and violet. Sunlight which is broken by a glass prism shows these same colors.

All the colors have different waves of light. The longest waves that we can see are the red rays. The shortest that we can see are the violet rays. The longer red waves move more slowly than the shorter violet waves.

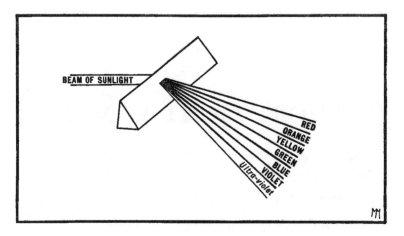

BEAM OF SUNLIGHT

RED
ORANGE
YELLOW
GREEN
BLUE
VIOLET
Ultra-violet

The ultra-violet rays are invisible.

We can see with our eyes the colors of broken light from red through orange, yellow, green, and blue to violet. We can see as far as violet, but we cannot see any color *beyond* the violet. Yet there are shorter, faster waves in sunlight than even the violet rays. We call them *ultra-violet* rays. (The word *ultra* means *beyond*.) We cannot see the ultra-violet rays. We say they are invisible.

Ultra-violet rays of sunlight are very important for us. They are good for growing children. They help, too, to keep grown people strong and well.

Boys and girls, and grown people too, living in the North do not always get as much ultra-violet light as they need in winter. They spend more time indoors in winter than in summer. And their bodies are covered with thicker clothes even when they are out in the sunshine. Rays of ultra-violet light do not pass readily through smoke. A very little smoke makes a great difference in the amount of light that can come through the air. For that reason people who live in cities where there is smoke cannot get as much benefit from sunshine as people living in the country.

There is a way, however, for people to get ultra-violet light even if they live in smoky cities; or if they live in the North, where winter days are short; or if they spend most of the time indoors.

Receiving the health rays from an ultra-violet lamp

Men who make different kinds of electric lamps have learned how to make lamps that give ultra-violet light. Schools in some places have rooms fitted with such lamps. The children stand near the lamps a short time each day so that the health rays can touch them. There are ultra-violet lamps in many hospitals and in some homes. Lights of this sort of course should not be used by anyone who has not learned how to use them properly.

You know that too much sunshine may harm you. Severe sunburns may be as troublesome as burns from a fire. You know, too, that you cannot look directly at the sun without hurting your eyes. And it is not safe to let ultra-violet light from a lamp shine directly into your eyes. There is also danger of "sunburn" if one of these lamps is used too often and too long.

When ultra-violet light touches the skin, it produces small amounts of a substance called *vitamin D*. Vitamin D helps bones to grow strong and helps keep them in good condition. All animals with bones need vitamin D in their bodies. One of the ways they can get it is by taking sun baths and receiving the ultra-violet rays of sunlight.

There is another way to get vitamin D. Some of this substance is in sardines, in salmon, in yolks of eggs, in butter, and in certain other foods. There is even more in cod-liver oil and halibut-liver oil. Many foods do not contain vitamin D naturally. Recently men have learned that, if they expose such foods to ultra-violet light, they will act the same as foods that have vitamin D.

The short ultra-violet rays of sunlight cannot pass through ordinary window glass. But a special kind of glass can be made through which these rays can pass. Some buildings are fitted with glass of this sort.

What To Do after Reading Chapter Twelve

BREAKING WHITE LIGHT

Did you ever use a piece of glass to break white light so that it showed its different colors? If you never did, read "Prisms and White Light" in "Robert's Science Party" in *Surprises*. Then make an experiment with a prism and white light.

WRITE

Write eight sentences, using one of the following words or expressions in each sentence:

(1) ultra-violet　　(5) sunlight

(2) light waves　　(6) rainbow

(3) vitamin D　　(7) invisible

(4) glass prism　　(8) sunburn

GUESS THIS RIDDLE

You'll find me in oil of salmon and cod.
Wherever the sun shines, you'll find me.
The alphabet has me—rhyming with T,
Rhyming with C and E, rhyming with Z.

MAKE A RIDDLE

Make a riddle of your own about one of the words or expressions you were asked to put into your eight sentences. Your riddle need not rhyme unless you like to have it.

CHAPTER XIII

THE LONGEST NIGHT

Twenty-four hours measure the length of one day and night. It makes no difference to the clock whether this day and night are in spring, summer, autumn, or winter. But during part of the year, more of these twenty-four hours have daylight; while during another part, more of the hours are dark.

A poet, Robert Louis Stevenson, stated this fact very well in lines with which you are perhaps familiar:

> In winter I get up at night
> And dress by yellow candle-light.
> In summer, quite the other way,
> I have to go to bed by day.

Why are winter days shorter than summer days? Why does the longest night come in December in the northern half of the earth?

We know that the earth is always moving, and that it has two kinds of motion.

Besides taking its daily spinning motion, the earth takes its yearly, or annual, journey around the sun. It is

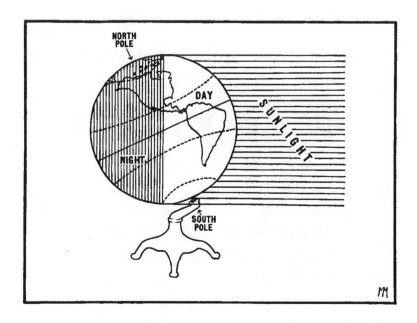

This is the position of the earth at the beginning of winter, when the north pole is tipped away from the sun and the south pole is tipped toward the sun.

Use a globe for the earth. Use a candle or an electric light for the sun. Turn the earth slowly around to see where night and day will be in winter. There will be no day at all at the north pole. There will be no night at all at the south pole. When the earth has traveled around to the other side of the sun, it will be summer. (See also page 110.)

during this long journey of four seasons that the changes occur in the amount of daylight and darkness.

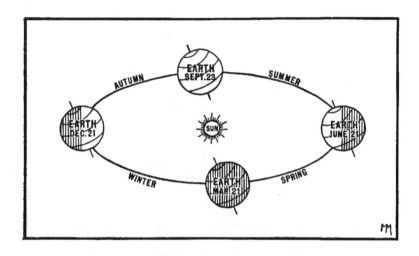

The annual journey of the earth

In spite of all the spinning and traveling the earth does, it never changes its position in any way with reference to the North Star, or polestar. As you have already learned from other books, this position remains the same at all times of the day and year. The north pole is turned toward the polestar while the earth spins like a top, making day and night. It is turned the same way while the earth travels in a circle around the sun, making spring, summer, autumn, and winter.

When the earth is on one side of the sun, the north pole is in the sunlight. We have our summer then. And when the earth is on the other side of the sun, the north pole is away from the sunlight. We have our winter then.

107

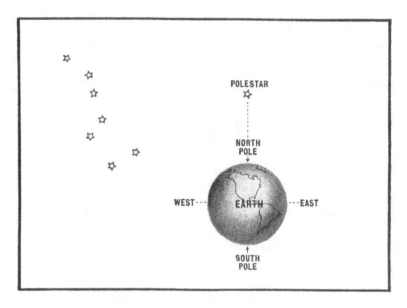

POLESTAR

NORTH POLE

WEST --- EARTH --- EAST

SOUTH POLE

The north pole is turned toward the polestar.

We call March 21 the beginning of real spring. Day and night are of equal length then.

Three months later, on June 21, the earth has traveled one quarter of the way around the sun. We call this day the beginning of real summer. We have the shortest nights and the longest days at this time of year, in the northern half of the world.

Real autumn begins September 23. The earth has taken half its journey around the sun by that time. The days and nights have the same length, just as they had at the beginning of spring.

We call December 21 the first day of real winter. At this time of year the nights are longest and the days are shortest in the northern half of the world. The earth is now opposite the place where it was six months before, at the beginning of summer. In three months more it will reach the place where it started on March 21.

It takes the earth twenty-four hours to spin once around like a top either in the winter or in the summer. But in the winter more of the hours are dark in the northern half of the world. So we say the winter nights are longer there.

In most parts of the world there is some sunlight even when the nights are longest. A part of every twenty-four hours is daytime. The farther north we go, however, the longer the winter nights become. At last, when we reach the north pole, we find that there is no daylight at all for three months.

The region near the north pole we call the arctic region. The long arctic night is not so dark as you might think. The stars are shining at all hours. The moon can be seen much of the time.

In the far North, too, the northern lights are brilliant. They are natural electric fireworks in the sky. Sometimes they look like thin white draperies floating in the air. Sometimes they move in streaks and bands. They often have yellow and red and green colors and make moving pictures of gorgeous light. Some people visit the far North for the purpose of seeing them. Northern lights can be seen on some winter nights in many parts of the United States, but they are not so splendid as they are in regions far to the north.

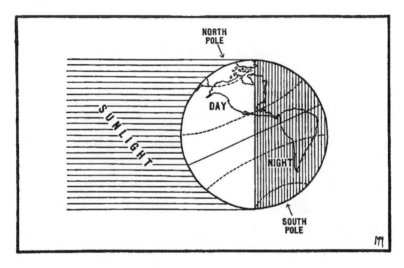

Northern days are longest in summer.

This is the position of the earth at the beginning of summer. The earth has now traveled halfway around the sun. The earth is on the side of the sun that is opposite the place where it was at the beginning of winter. (See page 106.)

Use a globe for the earth. Carry it in a circular path halfway around the sun (candle of electric light). Notice that the north pole is now tipped toward the sun. The south pole is tipped away from the sun. Spin the earth slowly to see where night and day come.

What To Do after Reading Chapter Thirteen

TRAVELING AROUND THE SUN

Use a darkened room. Place a lighted candle in the center of a round or oval table. Call the candle the sun.

Choose a spot at the top of one wall of the room to call the North Star.

Call a globe the earth. (If you have no globe, use an orange or ball. Put a knitting needle through it to show the north and south poles.)

Now take the earth on its journey around the sun. Keep the north pole always tipped toward the North Star.

Find out why the northern part of the earth is toward the sun during part of the journey. Find out why it is away from the sun part of the time.

READ

In the book *Introduction to World Geography*, read about Eskimos, the people of the arctic region (pages 187–195).

In the same book, read about the shape of the earth and about night and day (pages 18–21).

In "Earth, Sun, Moon, and Stars" in the book *Surprises*, read about our earth.

In the same chapter in *Surprises* read about the North Star.

WRITE

Write a few sentences about daylight and darkness early in each of two seasons, spring and autumn or summer and winter. Write your sentences in prose if you prefer. If you like to use rhyming words, as Robert Louis Stevenson did, you may write in verse form.

Write a few sentences about winter in the arctic region. Tell what lights may be seen there during the time of year when there is no daylight.

Perhaps you have heard the word *equinox*. This word is made from two Latin words, one meaning *equal* and the other meaning *night*. At the time of the equinox day and night have equal length; each is twelve hours long. There are two equinoxes each year. Write enough to tell in which month the equinox last occurred. Tell in which month the next equinox will be.

CHAPTER XIV

THE SEASONS IN SOUTH AMERICA

When does winter come in the southern part of South America? When would you see leafless trees if you were in Argentina?

There was once a boy living in Argentina who ran and played on the wide, level, grassy fields called the *pampas*. He rode on the pampas, too. He did not need to use a saddle. By the time he was six years old he could ride a bareback horse even when it was galloping very fast.

This boy loved the pampas. He visited the flowers and watched the birds there. Indeed, he was so very happy that he did not forget the colors and the fragrance of the flowers or the sound of the bird songs even after he grew to be a man and lived in another part of the world, for after a time he left South America and went to England to stay.

The boy's name was William Hudson. In this chapter you will be told a little about him and the place where he lived—far-away Argentina.

Some Argentina trees in December

There were few trees on the pampas themselves. But people planted trees around their homes. There were thousands of trees on the plantation where William lived. Some of them were old trees that had been set out more than one hundred years before. People who had come from Spain had put them there. They did not take wild trees from the wooded places in South America. They brought young trees from Spain so that they could have peaches and poplars and other kinds they had loved in their old homes.

None of these trees were evergreens. They dropped their leaves in the fall. Their branches were bare during May and June and July.

The peach trees blossomed in August. The flowers were so thick that they looked like fluffy pink clouds against the bright blue sky. That was the time, too, when the finches sang their spring songs. The finches were pretty little yellow birds that spent much time in the pampas. But in August they sat in the peach trees and sang together. So there were thousands of yellow birds singing among the millions of pink flowers.

In February the peaches on those trees were ripe. Then young William Hudson could have plenty of sweet, juicy fruit to eat.

After the peach trees were through blossoming, in August, their leaves began to grow and their branches were green instead of pink.

About the same time of year there were new leaves to watch on the willows, too. Willows grew near a stream that ran into the Plata River, not far from

Grass on the pampas

William's home. They grew there naturally. They had not been brought from Spain. They were called red willows because the rough trunks had a reddish color.

Long double rows of poplar trees had been planted on three sides of the plantation. The spring air was filled with the fragrance of young poplar leaves. William liked this odor so well that he crushed some of the tender leaves in his hands and rubbed them against his face.

The hottest summer days came in December and January. The trees had their leaves then, but there was not enough rain to keep the plants on the pampas growing. These vast plains became dry and brown and there was danger of fires. But in the late autumn and in winter and spring there was enough rain to keep water in the streams, and the grass and other plants were green and growing then.

Giant thistles grew on the pampas. Some years they were very thick indeed. They grew six to ten feet high, and their prickly leaves were as large as rhubarb leaves. There were other tall plants on the pampas. Wild deer could hide among the clumps. William often saw the deer when he rode on the pampas.

A rhea

One day when William was eight years old, he was sent to bring back a flock of sheep that had strayed too far. He mounted his pony and trotted across the pampas until he found them. The sheep were not alone. Many rheas were feeding near them. Rheas are giant running birds related to the ostriches that live in Africa. They are sometimes called South American ostriches. The rheas were not afraid of William. They looked at the young boy on his pony and went on eating clover that was growing near some prickly thistles.

William Hudson saw flamingos and parrots and many other kinds of birds while he was a boy in Argentina. Some kinds stayed near his home all through the year. Other kinds were migrants. They traveled north to a warmer part of South America to stay during the winter months.

What To Do after Reading Chapter Fourteen

CHOOSE THE RIGHT WORD

Copy the following sentences and put the right word in each blank space.

January	December	parrots
plantation	Argentina	May
June	prairies	peach
pampas	July	November

I wish I could visit a country called _____ in South America. I would look for some wide, grassy fields. I should not call them meadows or _____. I should call them _____.

There would be many strange birds there whose names I do not know. But I could tell _____ if I saw any because I have seen some in a zoo.

118

Most of the wild trees would be quite different from any I know in North America. But I could name some of the trees on a _____, because some of the same kinds are planted in orchards in North America. I could tell the _____ trees when the fruit was ripe.

It would seem strange to see poplar trees with bare branches in the months of _____ and _____ and _____. In North America these trees would have no leaves in _____ and _____ and _____.

USE AN INDEX

Turn to the index in the back of *Introduction to World Geography*. Look for the word *Argentina* in this index. You will find the numbers of seven pages after this word. Turn to each of these pages and read what is said there about Argentina.

COPY A MAP

Find a map of South America in a geography. Copy the outline of this map. Put in the country called Argentina. Draw the Plata River.

CHAPTER XV

SONG AND DANCE

Years ago in many countries there was a happy holiday every spring. The people of each village rose at dawn and gathered flowers and branches of trees. They marched with these to the center of the village, where they put up a tall pole gay with ribbons and wreaths. Then they danced in circles around the pole and sang.

There are still Maypole dances in some places; but there are not so many as there were once. People change their customs from time to time. They have different ways of showing that they are happy.

Birds, however, keep their customs from century to century. And one of the pleasant habits of many birds is to dance in the springtime.

> The birds around me hopped and played,
> Their thoughts I cannot measure:—
> But the least motion which they made
> It seemed a thrill of pleasure.

The four lines you have just read were written by a man named William Wordsworth. He wrote them in the early spring of 1798. That is not an important date for you to remember, for birds were acting just the same that spring as they had been acting for thousands and thousands of years.

Our American robins have loud songs that are well known to most people who have been in country places in the spring. They have, too, a different sort of song that not so many people have heard. This is the robin dance song, and one must be very near indeed to hear it. A dancing robin moves slowly back and forth along a branch, over and over again. And all the while he makes soft, low, murmuring music, not at all like his other songs. If his mate is near enough to hear him, she listens and watches as if she, too, were happy.

Flocks of purple finches sit in trees and sing together in spring. Often there will be more than twenty voices in a finch male chorus. They sing gaily during bright days when the sun is shining; and they sing just as cheerfully during gray days when the air is full of mist or drizzling rain.

But when they dance, each bird leaves the chorus. He finds a good place on the ground for his dancing floor. Then he spreads his wing feathers and his tail and takes pretty strutting steps. His throat puffs out and he sings all the while he dances. His music now is not like his chorus song. It is a special long, low, sweet warble that his mate likes best of all. She stands quite still and watches him and listens to his tune.

Have you ever seen a crow fly slowly over a field, calling, "Caw, caw, caw!" loudly and hoarsely as he goes? Perhaps you would never guess that a crow can sing and dance. But he can! He can dance a merry, sideling, hopping jig on the ground. And while he dances he sings a low tune quite softly. At such times his notes are what people call "liquid"—like a musical little brook bubbling over pebbles.

Every spring the tiny ruby-throated humming bird comes hundreds of miles from southern Florida or Louisiana or from Mexico to more northern places. He does not feel weary after his journey. He feels like singing and dancing. His song is a series of thin chattering squeaks, and his dance is in the air. He does not need the ground to step on, as does a strutting finch or a jigging crow. He does not even need a branch to rest on, as does a robin. The air is firm enough for him! There he swings in a curve about eight or ten feet across, going back and forth hundreds of times.

His wings whir too fast to be seen clearly.

And all the while another little humming bird, whose throat has no ruby feathers, is perched on a slender twig. She stays near enough to watch the quick-swung motions and hear the squeaking of this strange song and dance.

They were not American robins and purple finches and crows and humming birds that William Wordsworth saw that day in early spring when he wrote the poem you read at the beginning of this chapter. William Wordsworth lived in England, where most of the birds are different from those here. But in England and in the United States and in every other country the joy of birds is a glad part of springtime.

What To Do after Reading Chapter Fifteen

THE SAME NAME FOR DIFFERENT THINGS AND DIFFERENT NAMES FOR THE SAME THING

Sometimes the same name has been given to quite different things. William Wordsworth knew "robins" very well. But robins like those he saw in England are a different kind of bird from the robins you see in this country. English robins are little birds less than six inches in length. They build their nests in low places. Their eggs are white speckled with red. Their songs are not at all like the songs of the birds called robins in this country. Both kinds of robins, however, have red breasts.

English blackbirds belong to the Thrush Family.

They sing together in the early dawn. Some people think that a chorus of English blackbirds make the most beautiful bird music in the world. American blackbirds belong to the same family as orioles and bobolinks. Their habits are not like those of birds belonging to the Thrush Family.

Kerosene and *coal oil* are two names for the same kind of oil. *Checkerberry*, *ivory plum*, and *wintergreen* are three names for the same kind of fruit.

Talk with people you know and learn some different names for the same things. Learn about some different things that go by the same names. Make a list of such names as you find interesting. Talk about them with your teacher.

The sap flows before the leaves grow in the spring.

CHAPTER XVI

MAPLE SAP

A maple tree needs a great deal of water to keep it alive and growing. This water comes in through the roots. It passes up the trunk of the tree and along the branches into the leaves. Water escapes from the surface of the leaves in the form of vapor. Much of the moisture in the air is the vapor that comes from the leaves of trees and other plants.

There are minerals in the ground that the tree needs for its growth and health. Some of these minerals are mixed with the water that the roots take in. There are fine, long passageways in the trunk of the tree through which this water rises. They are sometimes called water tubes. The water rises as far as the highest branches and finds its way to all the leaves.

The leaves make sugar while the sun shines. The tree needs the sugar for food. There are passageways through which this food, dissolved in water, goes to the growing parts of the tree. This food water is the liquid we call sap.

The very center of the trunk of a tree is stiff wood that is no longer growing. It gives strength to the tree and is a sort of skeleton for it. All around this strong central part is a region that is alive and growing. It grows in circles or rings. Each year one new ring is formed outside all the others. If you look at the trunk of a tree that is cut across, you can count the rings and tell about how old the tree was when it was cut down.

Count the rings to see about how old the tree was.

The living part of the trunk is called *sapwood*. The water tubes through which the water rises are in the sapwood. There, too, are the passages through which the sugary water that comes from the leaves is carried to other growing parts of the tree. Some of the food sugar is used soon. Some of it is changed to starch and stored in tiny cells in the sapwood. Some of it remains there all winter. In the spring this starch is changed again to sugar and used for food by the leaves and other growing parts.

Some plants store starch in tubers, as potatoes do. Some store starch in bulbs, as lilies do. Each kind of plant has some way to store starch to use when it is most needed for growth. The tree, as you have just learned, stores starch in cells in the sapwood.

The trunk and branches have a covering that is called *bark*. The outer part of the bark is a hard protecting coat for the tree. It is not alive and growing. It cracks as the parts inside grow. You can see this thick, cracked outer bark on the trunks of old trees. The inner bark is soft and alive and growing.

All summer the maple roots are very busy taking in water from the ground. The big, thick, heavy roots cannot do this. It is only the slender growing white ends of the roots that can do this work for the tree. Near these root ends are great numbers of fine, white *root hairs*. The water in the soil is absorbed by the root hairs. As the roots grow, their tips push farther and farther into the soil. New root hairs keep growing near the root ends. So there are always plenty of them to get water for the tree.

During the summer the leaves and other living parts of the tree need water to use. In the fall the leaves drop from the maple tree. Then the tree needs no water for them. The cold weather arrives, and the tree becomes dormant. The root hairs take in very little water during the winter.

When spring rains come and the ground is wet, the

root hairs take in a great deal of water. The water rises and rises in the water tubes in the sapwood of the trunk. This begins to happen early in the spring—before the leaves in the buds start to grow. At this time the nights are cold though the sunny noons are warm. As the water rises in the sapwood it comes in touch with the starch that has been stored in the cells in the sapwood. The starch is changed to sugar, which sweetens the sap. This sweet food is all ready for the leaves. But the leaves are not yet ready for the food. The weather is not quite warm enough for them.

This is the time in the spring when people *tap* their maple trees. They cut holes through the bark and into the sapwood. They see the sap drip rapidly through these holes, and they say there is a good "flow of sap." They let it run from the holes into pails.

The sap is boiled in great kettles until much of the water goes off in vapor. After a time the sweet liquid in the kettles is thick enough for syrup. Some of it is put into jars or cans to be used as syrup. Some of it is left in the kettles and boiled until most of the water has passed away in vapor and the syrup has become sugar.

After a while the leaves of the maple tree start to grow. Then the sap no longer runs freely out of the holes. The little drops come very slowly. People say that the flow of sap is over. Of course the sap is still rising in the maple tree. But the leaves use it now.

Sap rises in other trees and bushes, as it does in maple trees. But the sap from the maple tree has more sugar than that from most other trees and bushes and it has a better flavor.

What To Do after Reading Chapter Sixteen

BLOOD AND SAP

Copy these two sentences and supply the right word for each space.

(1) There is a liquid that flows in the bodies of animals. It carries food to all the parts of the body that need it. The name of this liquid is _____.

(2) There is a liquid that carries food to the different growing parts of trees and other plants. Its name is _____.

SAP THAT GOES UP

The water that is absorbed by root hairs goes up to higher parts of the plants. Some of it goes to the very highest growing tips.

Put some mustard seeds between two pieces of damp blotting paper. Place the blotting paper in a covered dish. If the dish is glass, put it in the dark. Keep the blotting paper moist until the seeds have sprouted.

Look at one of the young mustard plants through a magnifying glass. Can you find fine, short root hairs on its root? Are these at the very tip of the root or back a little way?

Make a drawing to show the root and root hairs of a young mustard plant.

The many fine, long tubes in the body of a tree or other plant, reaching from the roots to the leaves, are sometimes spoken of as the *veins* of the plant. The fluid taken in by the roots goes *up* through these fine, long tubes.

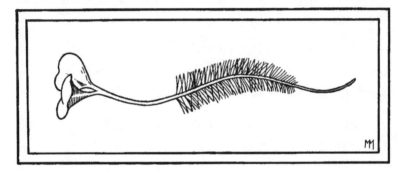

Write a short account of your young mustard plants, explaining how fluid from the moist blotting paper went from the root hairs to the new leaves. Use the word *veins* in your account.

SAP THAT GOES DOWN

In the spring of the year a tree begins to make new growth in its trunk and branches. A new layer is added to the *outside* of the sapwood. The bark has new growth on its *inside* part. A great deal of sap is poured *down* the tree between the sapwood and the bark, to be used in this new growth.

For a while in the spring this downward-moving sap makes a rather slimy layer under the bark. Then it is easy to remove the bark from a branch. This is the time to make willow whistles. If there is a willow tree from which you may cut branches, make a willow whistle at the right time in the spring.

Notice how easily the bark can be peeled from the branches of some other trees or bushes at this time.

SAP THAT GOES IN BRANCHED TUBES

There are branched tubes (or vessels) in the inner living part of the bark. These branched tubes take in some of the sap that goes down between the sapwood and the bark. After the sap is taken into these tubes, it becomes changed in different ways.

Look at the picture on this page. Then close the book and draw some branched tubes.

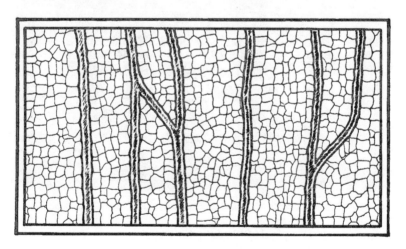

Tapping a rubber tree

CHAPTER XVII

TAPPING A RUBBER TREE

You have already learned that all the sap in trees does not move the same way. In the previous chapter you read about sap that goes up from the roots to the leaves. Next you read about sap that moves down between the sapwood and the bark. You also read a little about sap that moves through tubes that branch into one another. In this chapter you will read more about this sort of sap.

Do you think it is rather hard to remember about three kinds of saps? Perhaps it will help you if you have a different name for the third kind—the sap in branched tubes. You may call it *latex*. (The word *latex* means a liquid or a juice.) That is what people who study plants usually call it. Sometimes they use the name *latex tubes* or *latex vessels* for the branched tubes through which the latex flows.

Latex may differ from other sap in color or odor or taste. Very often it is as white as milk. So we speak of the "milky" juice of certain plants. The "milk," or latex, of some plants is bitter. Did you ever taste the juice that oozes from a torn dandelion stem? Some plants have latex that will burn your tongue like liquid fire if you taste it. A little latex from the opium poppy is enough to put a person to sleep. A large dose of it would kill one.

Although the latex of many plants is very disagreeable or even poisonous, it is not always like that. Indeed there is a kind of tree growing in South America that is called the *cow tree*. The "milk" of a cow tree has a pleasant taste and is a nourishing food. People tap such trees and use the latex to drink and in cooking.

The latex that is used most of all in the world is not a food. It comes from plants of the Spurge Family. This is a large family of plants. Most of them live in the warmest countries in the world, although a few of them live in colder climates. Some of our very common weeds are spurges. The plants with valuable latex, however, are not any of our northern weeds. They are tall relatives of theirs that live wild in South America. They are trees that sometimes grow to be more than one hundred feet high. They are known as *Hevea trees* or *rubber trees*.

When white men first visited South America, they found that the native people there had a jolly sort of ball game. Their balls bounced when they hit any hard surface, like the trunk of a tree or the ground. These bounding balls were made from the juice of Hevea trees. The juice is a milk-white latex. The natives heated it over their smoky fires to make it thick enough for balls. It turned dark in the smoke. The white visitors were very much interested in these balls. They took some home to Europe for children to play with.

For many years the latex of the Hevea trees had no more important work to do in the world than to serve as jumping balls in games. But after a time men found that this substance was useful in removing lead-pencil marks from paper. Men in English art shops named the stuff *rubber,* because it was so good to use to rub out lead marks. Soon everybody who wrote with lead pencils liked to have rubbers to use as erasers.

Most of the latex from rubber trees is now put to other uses than rubbing lead marks from paper, for people in different parts of the world learned to make more and more things of rubber. They learned to make so many things that it became rather difficult to get from South America all the rubber that was needed. So after a while seeds were collected from the wild trees. The young trees from these seeds were planted in other warm regions. They were put in rows and cared for. Today more rubber is obtained from cultivated Hevea trees in other countries than from wild trees in countries in South America.

You will remember that maple trees are tapped only in the late winter or very early spring. The clear sweet sap comes from the sapwood. Rubber trees are tapped every day in the year. The white sap comes from the latex tubes in the soft inner part of the bark.

When a man taps a rubber tree, he does not bore into the sapwood. He needs only to cut through the bark with a sharp knife, and juice runs out of the latex tubes. It is a very sticky juice, and after it has dripped for a while it forms a gummy scab over the wound.

A young rubber tree

Then no more latex can leak through. That is why it is necessary to tap a rubber tree each day. The tapping is done early in the morning because the latex flows better at that time.

The milk-white latex is collected in cups, which are emptied into pails. The full pails are sent to a factory as soon as possible.

At the factory the latex is treated with an acid or something else that will cause it to become about as thick as dough. This doughy latex is then rolled into thick or thin sheets.

The thick sheets are dried slowly in the smoke of wood fires for about two weeks. By that time the rubber has become blackened and is dry enough to send to factories in other parts of the world, where it is made into rubber boots and other rubber articles.

The thin sheets do not need the heat from a fire to dry them. They dry in the air and do not become black. They are straw colored when they are sent out to factories.

Hevea trees are not the only plants with a latex from which rubber can be obtained. The latex from certain fig trees can be used the same way. The rubber plant that some people like to keep in their homes is a relative of fig trees. When it is planted out of doors in a warm climate, it may grow to be a large tree. It is sometimes called the India-rubber tree. But although rubber can be obtained from many plants, the Hevea trees are the best yet known for this purpose. So most of our rubber supply still comes from these trees.

The India-rubber tree is a relative of fig trees.
This large India-rubber tree is growing in Florida.

What To Do After Reading Chapter Seventeen

A CHART

Ask for some old newspapers and magazines that you may cut. Look in these for pictures of things made from rubber. Cut out pictures of rubber things and paste them on a chart. See how many different interesting pictures you can find.

MILKY JUICE

Cut the leaves or stems of some common weeds. Make a list of the names of all the plants you find with white, milky juice.

MILKWEED JUICE

You would not care to drink the white juice of a milkweed plant. You might, however, find a use for it. If there is one of these plants growing near by, break off a leaf. See if the juice that oozes out is sticky enough to use for mucilage. Make some experiments with it to see how sticky it is.

Butterflies like to visit flowers with long tubes.

CHAPTER XVIII

FLOWERS AND INSECTS

Millions and millions of years ago there was a time when there were no orange trees or other flowering plants of the Rue Family. There were no peach or cherry or apple trees or other flowering plants of the Rose Family. Indeed, the earth was without all the plants that have flowers with showy *petals* and fragrant odors.

In those days there were plants that had no flowers. Such plants had no seeds, but they had spores as fine as dust. The spores were scattered by the wind. When they settled on the ground, they sprouted. We have flowerless plants with spores now. Ferns are such plants. You can see masses of rusty brown spores in little pocketlike spore cases on some fern leaves, or *fronds*.

In the far-away ages there were trees and other plants that had flowers, but the flowers were without petals. The flowers had *stamens* and *pistils*. *Pollen* grew on the stamens. The pollen was blown about by the wind, and some of it reached the pistils in other flowers on the same kind of plant. Then a grain of pollen grew down through a part of the pistil until it came to a seed

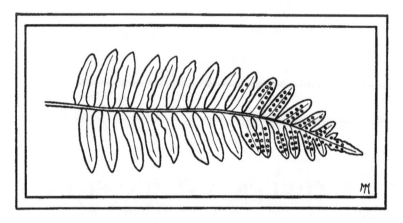

Ferns have tiny spore cases filled with spores.

that was just beginning to form. No seed could develop unless it was joined by a grain of pollen.

We have plants with petal-less flowers now. Most of them need the wind to blow the pollen from the stamen of one flower to the pistil of another flower. If you look at the flowers of pine or other cone-bearing trees or the flowers of birch trees or alder shrubs or grass, you will see that they grow on the plants where the wind can reach them and carry their pollen.

Men have a way of learning that some kinds of animals and plants were living on the earth before some other kinds. They learn this by studying the fossils they find in rocks.

If you take some soft clay and press a leaf into it, the form of the leaf will show even after the clay is dry and hard. You can make such impressions of plants or feathers or other things in clay.

There are impressions of plants and bodies of animals in rocks. Sometimes the hardened parts of plants are found. So are the bones of animals. Ages ago, when the rocks were being formed in layers and were becoming hard, plants and animal bodies were often buried in them and pressed. Many such remains or their impressions can be found in hard rocks. They are the fossils. Fossils may be hundreds or thousands or even millions of years old. The oldest rocks have the oldest fossils.

Elm flowers have no large bright petals.
The wind carries their pollen for them.

Looking at fossils is like looking at pictures of parts of animals and plants that lived on the earth long ago. Some of the same kinds or similar kinds still live here. Other kinds we know nothing about except what we can learn from their fossils.

147

The men who have studied fossils have found that there were plants with petal-less flowers on earth long before there were plants whose flowers have lovely white or colored petals. These men have learned, too, that there were insects living on the earth even in those ages when the flowers had no petals.

A fern fossil

Something remarkable has happened to many plants and insects since the time of the oldest fossils. In some wonderful ways many kinds of insects and many kinds of plants have grown to be partners. They help each other.

Insects carry pollen for certain plants. Many flowers are shaped so that the wind cannot reach their pollen. Only insects can get it and carry it for them. For this reason such plants owe their own lives and the lives of their seed children to insects.

In return for this benefit, great numbers of plants are very helpful to insects. Their flowers have more pollen than the plants need for their seeds. There is enough for insect guests to eat. Some bees, too, gather pollen and use it as food for their young.

Flowers do not need nectar for themselves. It is a pleasant treat for insects. While the insect guests are drinking nectar, their bodies brush against some of the pollen grains. The pollen sticks to them and is carried to other flowers that they visit.

Plants do not need fragrance for their own use. They cannot smell it. But insects like the odors of flowers. The odors are carried by the air. The insects smell them and fly to the flowers. The fragrance of flowers is an invitation to insects to come for a visit.

The colors of flowers give no pleasure to plants. They cannot see color. But insects see the colors of flowers. The flowers look different from the green leaves. So the white and colored petals are signs to tell insects, "This is the way to nectar or pollen."

Roses and some other flowers that have no nectar are supplied with a great deal of pollen for the insects that visit them.

Flowers that have nectar hold it in little tubes where insects can get it. In some flowers the tubes are not deep. Insects with short tongues can reach it. The tubes of some flowers are so deep that only insects with long tongues can drink the nectar.

Honeybees can reach the nectar of white clover, but they cannot drink from red clover. Their tongues are not long enough to reach the bottom of the red-clover tubes.

A bumblebee can get nectar from red clover.

Bumblebees are larger than honeybees and they have longer tongues. Bumblebees and red-clover plants are partners. Bumblebees benefit these plants by carrying pollen. So bumblebees benefit the cows and horses and other animals that eat clover. And they benefit the men who buy or sell clover for hay.

Butterflies and many moths have long tongues. An insect of this sort can stretch its tongue out straight and sip nectar much as you can suck lemonade through a straw. Then the tongue can be rolled into a coil, to be out of the way when the insect is not drinking.

Some plants keep their nectar for insects that fly after dark. They usually have white or pale yellow petals that show at night. These flowers pour forth a strong

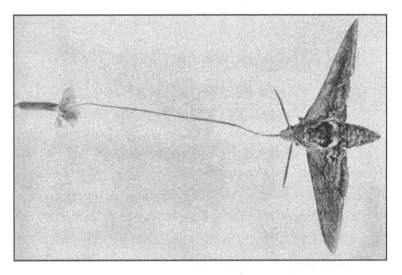

This moth's tongue is more than twice as long as its body.

perfume in the evening but are not so fragrant during the daytime.

Not all kinds of insects visit flowers. But, besides the insects already mentioned, many kinds of flies do; and some beetles are flower insects, too.

The next time you visit some flowers in a garden or orchard, or park or field, notice whether they have insect guests. You will find it interesting to see which flowers and insects are partners. Some flowers have such queer shapes that it is like a puzzle to guess how insects can reach their nectar. If you watch the right insect, it will give you a correct answer to the puzzle.

What To Do after Reading Chapter Eighteen

POLLEN INSECTS AND
THE COTTON PLANT

Did you ever try to think how people could get along without help from certain insects? Many plants depend upon pollen-bearing insects for their lives— they could have no seeds unless insect guests carried the pollen from flower to flower. Choose just one kind of plant and think about that.

The cotton plant would be a good one to think about. Insects carry cotton pollen and make cotton seeds possible. Men get many useful products from this plant.

Read "The Cotton Plant," Chapter VI in *First Lessons in Nature Study*. Read "How We Make Cloth Out of Plants," Chapter 13 in *First Lessons in Geography*.

Make a list of all the products you can learn about that people owe to the cotton plant.

Make a list of cotton products that you remember you have used yourself.

Think about people who make money from cotton. Here are six classes of people who have pollen-bearing insects to thank for all or part of their money. Why?

(1) Owners of cotton fields

(2) Laborers in cotton fields

(3) Owners of cotton mills

(4) People who work in cotton mills

(5) Owners of dry-goods stores

(6) Clerks at counters where things made from cotton are sold

See how many more classes you can add to this list.

Sphinx moth and evening primrose—a night flower
for a night insect

POLLEN INSECTS AND FRUIT

Would you rather think about fruit than cotton? If so, you may list classes of people who make money in some form of fruit business. You may find it interesting to see how many classes owe part of their money to insects that carry pollen for fruit trees and other fruit plants. Perhaps you will be surprised to see how long a list you can get for the apple, or the blueberry or some other juicy fruit.

Most of our juicy fruits are possible because their flowers are visited by pollen bearers. Read about those that are mentioned in "Juicy Fruits" in "Some Food from Plants" in *Surprises*.

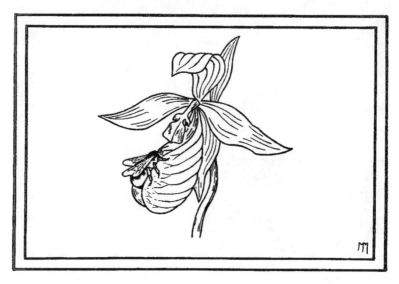

The bee creeps inside to get nectar from this flower.

CHAPTER XIX

THE SUN, THE MOON, AND THE FISH

Every spring the sun and the moon together help some fishes when they are ready to lay their eggs. That seems surprising, doesn't it? Very often facts are stranger than fairy stories.

The sun is about 93,000,000 miles away from the fishes, and the moon is about 240,000 miles away from them. How can they help some little fishes, called American smelts, that live in the Atlantic Ocean?

When the smelts are ready to lay their eggs, they leave the ocean and go as far as the tidewater reaches. But ordinary tides do not go far enough up into the streams. The smelts need a very high tide indeed. So they wait until the sun and the moon are pulling together. Then there is a *flood tide;* and a flood tide is what the smelts need each spring at egg-laying time.

You see, then, that, before you can understand how the sun and the moon help the smelts, you will need to learn a little about tides.

Low tide

TIDES

If you throw a stone up into the air, it soon falls to the ground. The earth pulls it down. If you tie one end of a string to the stone and then whirl the stone around in a circle, it does not fall as long as you keep it whirling. But as soon as it stops whirling it drops toward the ground.

The earth pulls the moon, but the moon does not fall into the earth. It is whirling around the earth too fast. The sun pulls the earth, but the earth does not fall into the sun. It is whirling too fast.

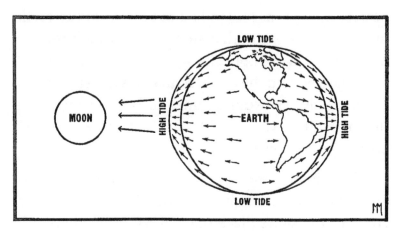

The moon and the tides

Everything pulls everything else. The earth pulls the moon, and the moon pulls the earth. The pull of the moon is so strong that the side of the earth that is nearest the moon bulges toward the moon a little. The rocks and the ground are too solid and stiff to bend much. You cannot notice any movement in them.

This slight movement can be measured only by a very sensitive instrument. Water, however, is loose and free to move. The moon can pull that much farther. It can pull the ocean so far that the water can be seen to go up and down.

Everyone who visits the seashore can notice that the water is high on the beach part of the time. Then much of the sand and many of the stones on the shore are covered with water. Part of the time the water is low, and then more of the sand and the stones on the shore are bare. It is this rise and fall of the water that we call the tide.

The tide is high on the side of the earth that is nearest the moon. It is pulled out ahead of the earth toward the moon on that side. At the same time the tide is high on the opposite side of the earth. On that side it lags behind the earth, so that it is high there, too. There are always two high tides and two low tides on the earth. The two high tides are opposite each other. So are the two low tides.

Since it takes the earth twenty-four hours to whirl around once, you might think that a high tide would come to the same place once every twelve hours. It does come almost as often as that. It is twelve hours and twenty-five minutes from the time one tide is at its height to the time when the next tide is at its height.

This chapter tells only the simplest facts about tides. There are other more complicated facts about them in other books. When you are older you will doubtless like to read more about tides. One of the facts you will

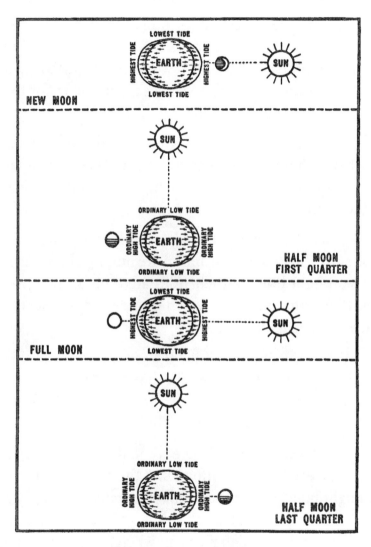

When are the tides highest

like to read about is why the high tides are not exactly twelve hours apart when it takes the earth twenty-four hours to make its day-and-night whirl.

You have learned that the pull of the moon makes tides in ocean waters. So does the pull of the sun. The sun is larger than the moon. It would make much bigger tides if it were as near the earth as the moon is, for the nearer a thing is, the stronger pull it has.

Although there are two high tides and two low tides each day, they are not always the same. At certain times each month the high tides are higher than they are at other times.

When the moon is "new," it is between the earth and the sun. The sun and the moon are pulling at the earth in a straight line. So their tides are high at the same time, and that makes a very high tide indeed. Such a tide is called a flood tide.

When the moon is "full," it is on the opposite side of the earth from the sun. The sun and the moon are pulling in a straight line then, too. So there is a flood tide when the moon is full, as there is when it is new.

What happens when there is a "half" moon? At that time the earth and the moon and the sun are not in a straight line. So the moon pulls the water at one place and the sun pulls it at another. Then of course the high tide cannot be so high as it can when the sun and the moon pull together.

This is high tide when there is a half moon. When the moon is full, the water, at high tide, covers all the ground as far up as the woods.

SMELTS

There are different kinds of fishes that belong to the Smelt Family. They are all small fishes with long pointed heads and wide mouths.

The Pacific smelt is found near the coast all the way from California to Alaska. It is about eight or nine inches long. The surf smelt, which grows to be about a foot long, is one of the largest members of the family. This also is found along the Pacific coast.

One kind is called rainbow herring, although it belongs to the Smelt Family instead of the Herring Family. This smelt has pretty purple, blue, violet, gold, silver, green, and rosy colors. It lives in the Bering Sea. The pond smelt lives in the Bering Sea, too. It goes to fresh-water ponds to spawn.

There are a number of kinds of smelts other than those mentioned. The kind we wish to tell most about in this chapter is called the American smelt.

American smelts live along the Atlantic coast from Virginia northward to the Gulf of St. Lawrence. They stay most of the time in the ocean near the coast. At certain times, however, they may be found in rivers and brooks, where they go to spawn. They stay rather near the mouths of these streams, going in and out with the tides. They do not, as a rule, go far enough to get into fresh-water ponds. In this respect their journeys differ from those of salmon, an account of which is given in another chapter.

If you would like to watch some of these fish in spring, you will find certain parts of the Maine coast good places to visit. The men who live there will tell you: "The smelts run in and out with the tides for about two weeks every spring. If you wish to see a great many of them, wait until the flood tide of the full May moon. That is the night when there is the heaviest run of all."

When this flood tide comes, it first covers the sea-shore with water. Next it rises high enough to cover the muddy flat places back from the shore. Then it goes higher yet between the banks of the streams. So instead of fresh water rushing down the streams, there is salt water rushing up the streams. The fresh water and the salt water meet farther and farther up. In some places the water overflows the banks and floods the land that is near.

It is rather jolly to run along the banks of one of these streams the night of a flood tide. It is fun to see the water from the ocean going up between the banks where, a few hours before, the fresh water was going the other way. But the most exciting part of it all is to see the smelts come up with the tidewater. They swim together in groups. The groups are called *schools*. There are often hundreds of the fish in one school.

You can see by the moonlight that something is moving in a brook where the water is not too deep. But you need a lantern or a flash light to see what the fishes are really doing. Then you can tell that they gather close to the stones in the water. That is where they spawn.

If you pick up one of these stones, you will find that

it is covered with tiny eggs, thousands and thousands of them. Each egg is about as large as a period on this page. There is a sort of glue mixed with the eggs in the mother fish's body. She pours out the glue with her eggs. When they touch the cold stone, they stick to it.

After the tide has reached its height, it turns. Then the water gets lower in the streams. The floods drain off the muddy flats. The tide sinks farther and farther down the seashore. At last it is low tide. The flood tide of the night of the full May moon is over, and most of the smelts are back again in the cove.

Most of the smelts that come up with a tide go back with the same tide. Sometimes, however, a school will linger in some sluggish place in a stream and stay there until a later tide. They are much more abundant at night, though often a few can be found by day. Then it is easier to see them.

American smelt

An American smelt is usually about eight or ten inches long. It has black eyes with silver rims. Its back is dull, soft green. Along the sides of the body next the green there is a streak of violet color. The rest has a silvery sheen. The fins are small and dainty. Some of them are shaped a little like the delicate wings of a May fly. They do not look strong, but the smelt darts very quickly in the water.

The falls at low tide

The smelt eggs need no care from the parent fish. They stick to the stones until they hatch. Then the tiny fish stay in the streams until they are old enough to go out to sea.

Of course the smelts cannot study about tides. They do not need to learn. They run in schools to spawn naturally, when the time of the year and the tides are right.

It is pleasant that people have studied tides and have learned so much about them. And it is rather interesting (don't you think?) to know that the sun, millions of miles away, and the moon, thousands of miles away, pull together and make a flood tide that helps the smelts at spawning time!

What To Do after Reading Chapter Nineteen

USE A MAP

In Chapter Nineteen you have read about some places where different kinds of smelts live. Look on a map to find just where these places are.

HOW DOES THE TIDE HELP ALEWIVES?

Look at the picture on the previous page. It shows a waterfall. The water falls from a fresh-water stream into salt ocean water. Every spring fish called *alewives* go from the ocean up these falls to find fresh water at spawning time. When the tide is "out" (or low), the falls are too high for the alewives to climb. They cannot leap like salmon. Explain what happens to these falls when the tide is "in" (or high). How does the tide help the alewives get over these falls?

Read "Visitors from the Sea," a chapter in *Holiday Pond.*

CHAPTER XX

FOOD FOR HUNGRY PLANTS

Plants need food to use as soon as they begin to grow in the spring. Most plants have some starch stored away ready to change to sugar. Sugar is a most important food for plants. As you have learned, they make it themselves in their green leaves.

You know that there is starch in different parts of plants:

In seeds, as in corn

In tubers, as in white potatoes

In bulbs, as in onions and many other members of the Lily Family

In cells in sapwood, as in trees

Such stores of starch are ready for the plants to use for their first food in spring. It lasts until the plants have started to grow and their leaves are ready to make more starch.

How can they get anything to make into new starch? You take food materials into your body through your mouth. Of course plants must get substances that are

Putting food on the ground for the corn plants

outside their bodies and take them into their bodies, too.

Plants take their materials through their roots, as you know, and through their leaves if they have roots and leaves. They take liquid with their roots and gas with their leaves.

There are some gases in the air that green leaves can take and use. Oxygen is one of these gases. This is the gas you take into your lungs when you respire, or breathe. Plants also take in oxygen when they respire.

Another gas that plants can take and use is *carbon dioxide.* You let this same gas out of your lungs when you respire. Plants use carbon dioxide when the sun shines, to make sugar in their leaves.

The air has one gas, however, that plants need but that their leaves cannot get for them. The name of this gas is *nitrogen.* About four fifths of the air is nitrogen. So you see there is much more of this gas than of any other in the air. The green leaves touch it all the time; but they cannot take any of it—not even if the plants are starving for it.

Air is mixed with the soil; so there is nitrogen gas in the ground around the roots. But the roots cannot take in this gas. They can absorb only substances that are dissolved in water, and the nitrogen gas does not dissolve in water.

What can the poor plant do? It will starve to death if it does not have nitrogen to use. There is plenty of this gas in the air touching its leaves and in the ground near its roots; but it cannot get it into its body.

If, however, the nitrogen combines with another substance to make something that can dissolve in water, then the roots can get hold of it. That is just what happens. It is not easy, to be sure, for nitrogen to combine with anything else. This is the reason why there is so much of it in the air.

There are three ways by which nitrogen can occur in the soil in forms that can be used by plants.

When old wood and leaves decay,
they make good food for plants.

When any plant or animal substance decays, it gives off nitrogen. But this nitrogen is not like the free gas form in the air. It is combined with other things in a form that can be dissolved in water. So one way the roots can get hold of nitrogen is to take it from something that is decaying. There are nearly always some such substances in the soil or on top of it. For one example, all the leaves that drop to the ground in the fall decay and help make nitrogen combinations that dissolve in water. Decaying bark and stems and branches help, too.

Lightning forces gases in the air to combine.

Rain and snow bring nitrogen to plants. The two gases nitrogen and oxygen do not usually have anything to do with each other while they are in the air. They are simply mixed together very much as you might mix together two kinds of seeds or sand and sugar. They do not combine and make a different substance. The great electric sparks of lightning, however, can force these gases to combine. The new substance that these gases make when they combine is an acid which dissolves in water. Raindrops wash this acid out of the air to the ground. Rain or melting snow washes it into the soil, and the roots get out of the acid a little of the nitrogen that is in it.

Another form of nitrogen which will dissolve in water is *ammonia*. This is also a gas. It sometimes escapes into the air when animal or vegetable matter is decaying. It may also come from burning coal. Rain and snow wash some of the ammonia out of the air. It soaks into the soil, and the roots get some nitrogen from the ammonia that is dissolved in the water they absorb.

So you see that the second way plants get some nitrogen is from acid and ammonia that are washed from the air into the soil.

The third way is the most important of all. There are great numbers of bacteria in the soil—millions and billions and trillions of them! A bacterium, you remember, is a tiny living organism with only one cell in its body. You read about certain bacteria in the second chapter of this book. Many kinds are exceedingly helpful to other living things. Different kinds of helpful bacteria work in the soil.

Soil bacteria can take nitrogen gas from the air and force it to combine with other things to make *nitrates*. The bacteria are as powerful in this respect as lightning is. Although bacteria are so small that you cannot see them unless you look at them through a microscope, yet they can get hold of nitrogen in ways that plants with green leaves cannot do.

Most of the helpful soil bacteria thrive best in places where there is plenty of *humus*. By *humus* we mean decayed materials in the soil. *Leaf mold* is one common sort of humus.

The nitrates which bacteria help make in the soil are useful to all leafy plants. They dissolve in water; so they can be absorbed by the roots of these plants.

As the water soaks through the ground into hollows or streams, however, it takes the nitrates with it. A great deal of the nitrogen is thus taken away from the soil by the water. Much of it is wasted in places where plants cannot get it with their roots.

There are certain plants, however, that have a sort of partnership with some kinds of bacteria. These are beans and peas and clover and peanuts and other

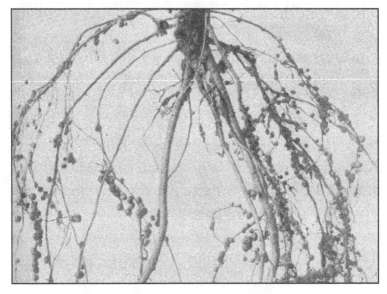

The soy bean belongs to the Pulse Family.
Notice the wartlike lumps on the roots.

plants belonging to the same family. This large family is sometimes called the Pea Family and sometimes the Pulse Family.

Colonies of bacteria live together in little wartlike lumps on the roots of these plants. The lumps are called *nodules*. The bacteria in the nodules get some food from the roots of the plants. And the roots get nitrogen food made by the bacteria. Thus the bacteria and the plants of the Pulse Family help each other constantly.

Such plants take a great deal of nitrogen. They put much of it into their seeds. You get some of this substance if you eat baked beans or pea soup or peanuts.

Soil in which members of the Pulse Family grow becomes rich in nitrogen. That is one reason why farmers like to grow clover on their land. Then they plow the land and use it for plants that do not have bacteria nodules on their roots.

Plants would probably get all the nitrogen they need if all the nitrogen combination (formed in the presence of humus and bacteria and washed from the air by rains) stayed in the soil until it could be used. But, as has been explained, the rains that soak through the ground wash away a great deal of it. Most plants, except members of the Pulse Family, often need more nitrogen than they can get. Plants, indeed, may starve and die if a farmer tries to grow crops on his land, year after year, without giving them nitrogen in some form they can use.

How can a farmer get nitrogen for his crops? He can add humus to his land. That helps in two ways.

The humus itself is good for the plants. Also, it makes a home for soil bacteria. There are many decayed substances that make good humus. Leaf mold has been mentioned. Barnyard manure is valuable in this connection. It has good nitrogen compounds in it that the plants can use.

The farmer can grow clover or some other member of the Pulse Family every few years. You already know that soil in which such plants grow becomes rich in nitrogen.

Chemists have learned how some of the nitrogen in the air can be combined with the gas called *hydrogen*. This is done in great factories, where the hydrogen is obtained by passing steam through red-hot coke. This hydrogen is then used with nitrogen to form ammonia. Forms of nitrogen can be made so cheaply in factories that farmers can afford to buy them to use for plant food.

There are nitrate foods, though, that men do not make in factories. One kind comes from mines in a desert. This desert is in the driest part of Chile in South America. The nitrate is found there in great quarries. It does not dissolve in the quarries because little or no rain falls on it and no other water touches it. For many years nitrate dug there has been sent to farmers all over the world.

The boy whose picture is shown on page 168 of this book lives in the United States. He is using some nitrate from Chile. He takes it out of the pail and puts it on the ground. That is the way he feeds nitrogen to

Getting nitrate in a desert in Chile

his corn. When the next rain comes, the nitrate will dissolve in the rain water and soak into the ground, where the corn roots can get it.

You have read in this chapter chiefly about one kind of food that plants need. They take many other foods besides nitrogen. Wild plants grow in places where the soil has what they need. Some kinds of plants are found in certain soils. Other kinds live in different soils. The farmer, however, uses the same ground over and over again for only a few kinds of crops. So he needs to add food to his soil to take the place of what his crops have used.

There are two kinds of food besides nitrogen (in nitrates) that the farmer most often puts in his soil. These are *phosphorus* and *potassium*.

There is some of both these substances in rocks.

When rocks crumble, some of these foods mix with the soil where the plants can use them. Certain rocks are taken to factories and treated with chemicals. This changes the phosphorus in them to a form the plants can easily use. Potassium compounds (potash) are taken from mines. Some of these mines are in Europe. There are also some in the United States. Much potash is taken from the dry bed of what was once a huge lake in California.

Crumbling rocks

Nitrates and phosphorus and potash are fertilizers. *To fertilize* means *to make fertile*. Fertile ground bears large crops. So you see *fertilizer* is a good name for these plant foods.

What To Do after Reading Chapter Twenty

PLANT FOOD

Put some sand in a fine sieve and let water run through it. The water will wash away what plant food it can dissolve. Then fill two flowerpots with the sand.

Put no fertilizer in one pot. In the other pot put a teaspoonful of fertilizer that has some nitrate and phosphorus and potassium. (A little of this can be bought already prepared.)

Plant the same kind of seeds in both pots. (Corn or beans will sprout quickly.)

After the plants have been growing for a while, draw a picture showing both pots and the plants in them. Under the picture, tell which pot had fertilizer.

CHAPTER XXI

THE PRESIDENT'S SALMON

There is a salmon pool in the Penobscot River at Bangor, Maine. The first salmon taken each year in this pool is sent to the President of the United States.

In another chapter of this book you read about smelts that come into the streams at high tide to spawn. They often come only a short way up the streams. They do not usually stay long before going back to the ocean. They are ready to lay their eggs the first day they come.

Salmon, as you know, do not spawn until the weather becomes cool. They do not wait until fall, however, to leave the ocean and swim up the rivers. They start their fresh-water journeys in the spring of the year.

The word *salmon* means *leaper*. There is a good reason why these fish were given this name. They are famous jumpers. When they reach falls in the rivers, they leap up over the falls and then go on swimming upstream.

In the old days these fish never had much trouble getting up most of the rivers they entered far enough to

A salmon for the President

find good places to put their eggs. They could not jump up over the very high Niagara Falls, but they could find places in most falls where they could get over the top.

Men began to build dams. After that the salmon could no longer get to many of their spawning places. The dams were smoother than the falls and their edges were more even. There were no rough jutting places from which the salmon could leap. There were no natural fishways in this new kind of waterfall.

Of course if the salmon could not get to their spawning places, they could not lay their eggs where the young fish could live and grow. If the old salmon could not go up a river, there would be no young salmon to come down this river to the sea. If there were dams in all the rivers, there would be no migrating salmon at all. Then there would be only the small landlocked salmon that stay in the lakes where they spawn.

As soon as dams were built in rivers, people began to worry about the salmon and other migrating fishes. So laws were passed in the different coast states to help the fishes. The laws declared that fishways must be built at all dams where fish are allowed to go. In Maine, for example, a state officer (the Commissioner of Inland Fisheries) may require the owner of a dam to provide the dam with a "durable and efficient fishway."

Just above the Bangor Salmon Pool there is a dam across the Penobscot River. The salmon used to try to get over this dam at migration time. They leaped and threw themselves against it until they became too weary to move. To be sure, there is a fishway at this dam. It was a "durable" fishway. Its foundations were put down about sixty feet, and it was a very strong concrete structure. But it was not an "efficient" fishway. The salmon were not able to use it. So the Bangor Pool was a sort of salmon trap. The fish did not have a chance to get up the Penobscot River to their spawning places.

Bangor Salmon Pool and dam

Of course the owners of the dam did not intend to cheat the fish or evade the law when they had this fishway built. Perhaps the person who planned the fishway did not know enough about the movements of fishes to draw the right sort of plan. It may be rather easy to make mistakes when building fishways. There have been a number of the wrong kind built in different rivers in Maine—fishways that are "durable" but not "efficient."

What would you do about a dam with a useless fishway if you were a Commissioner of Inland Fisheries? Would you require a new and proper one to be built? Perhaps you would like to know what was done about the fishway above the pool where the President's salmon is caught each spring.

The Commissioner and certain Congressmen visited this fishway to examine it. Soon after that visit a Bangor paper reported, "It is proposed to blast out the ledge and rocks below the fishway to permit of a free access of salmon, by changing the current of the water pouring over the dam."

The huge ledge prevented salmon from getting up the fishway. This ledge has now been blasted out. The picture on the next page was taken while the blasting was going on. You can see the rocks and water thrown up by the explosion.

Clearing the path for the salmon

What To Do after Reading Chapter Twenty-One

DO FISH RECEIVE CARE IN YOUR STATE?

There are fish hatcheries in different parts of Maine. In the one pictured on the opposite page, there are concrete tanks with open sides. Fresh water runs through the tanks. Salmon are kept here while they are young.

Find out whether there are any fish hatcheries in your state. If there are, find out what kind of fish are hatched in them.

Is there a Fish Commissioner in your state? If there is, find out a little about his duties.

Are there fishways in rivers in your state? If there are, find out one or more kinds of fish that go through them.

Visit a fishway or a fish hatchery if you can.

A fish hatchery in Maine

CHAPTER XXII

SUMMER CLOUDS

There are often clouds in the sky at any season of the year, but summer is the time when you may be most interested in them. You are likely to be out of doors more during warm vacation days. So you see a great deal of the summer sky.

Some morning you may be planning to go on a picnic and you wonder what the weather will be. Then you ask an older friendly person, "Do you think it will rain?"

What will he do before he answers you? He will look at the sky. Perhaps it is a very dull morning, and the mist is so thick you can hardly see where the sun is. You may be surprised when your friend replies, "I think the sky will soon be clear, and that it will be a good day for a picnic."

Maybe the sun will be bright and much of the sky deep, clear blue. You may see some beautiful clouds that look like great fluffy white mountains with dark places in them here and there. Then you may be surprised to hear your friend say: "Those clouds are thunderheads. If I were you, I'd not have a picnic today!"

If we study the summer sky, we notice that there are certain forms of clouds which we see most often. Names have been given these clouds.

One form has a name that means a *curl*. The curly clouds are high in the sky. They are thin and white and dainty and are often shaped like wavy wisps of hair.

High curly clouds

Another form has a name that means a spread or a *layer*. A layer cloud looks like a sheet spread over parts or all of the sky. Clouds of this sort are nearer the earth than other kinds. They are not so far away as the high curly clouds. Very often layer clouds may be seen like a fog that has lifted to cover the lower part of the sky. Such layer clouds are frequent in fine weather. Then they are present most often in the morning and evening, for they disappear in the heat of the day. At other times layer clouds may be dark and rain may pour down from them.

One kind of cloud has a name that means a *heap*. Clouds of this sort are the fleecy, white, rolling clouds shaped like rounded heaps or mounds. We often see them when the sun is shining and most of the sky is blue. They are often such beautiful clouds that artists like to paint pictures of them. Many people, too, are glad to have pictures of these clouds in photographs that they take.

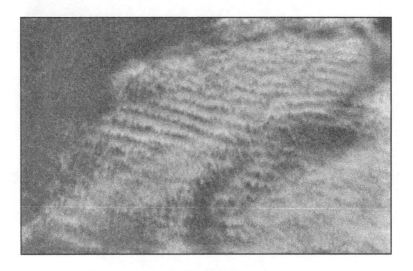

Sailors call it a "mackerel sky."

Sometimes you can see but one kind of cloud in the sky. Often, however, different kinds are mixed. Thin, wispy, curly clouds may thicken to form small white mounds. Then you see a mixture of clouds that you may think of as curly-mounds. The curly-mounds are moved by high air waves and usually appear in rows. Sailors have a name for a sky covered with such clouds.

They call it a "mackerel sky." (A mackerel is a fish with rows of wavy streaks on its back.)

Sometimes mound clouds look like huge rounded mountains and have dark layer clouds near them. People watch such mound-layer mixtures with much interest. They call these clouds thunderheads if the layer parts grow darker and larger.

Thunderstorm

The big white clouds are blown ahead by the wind. Darker and darker clouds follow. Lightning may begin to flash in the distance and a sound of far thunder may be heard. If the wind is blowing the clouds in your direction, you are soon in the midst of a thundershower.

Perhaps, however, the rain clouds are not over you. Then you can see the storm at a distance. The rain falls only on whatever is directly under a rain cloud. If you happen to be under the edge of the cloud, you can see the place where the shower begins or ends. When the edge of a rain cloud is over a house, the yard in front of the house may be wet and the back yard may be dry! Some summer day you may be on a hill in the bright sunshine while a little way off you can watch the rain pouring down from a black cloud.

You know that there is water in the air in the form of vapor. Clouds are made from droplets of this water. Or, when the air about the clouds is freezing cold, tiny ice crystals are formed instead of water droplets. These may become larger and fall as snowflakes. Hail is a mixture of frozen raindrops and snow.

There is dust as well as moisture in the air. Wind blows dust from the surface of the ground and from objects near the ground. That is how most of the dust gets into the lower air.

A great deal of dust goes higher into the air with smoke. Smoke of course may come from a small fire in a cigar, a fire in a factory furnace, a jolly bonfire, or many other kinds of fires. Sometimes so much smoke from a forest fire or a prairie fire stays high in the air that the daylight is changed even a long, long way from the fire. The smoke dust from such a fire may be in clouds or higher than the clouds. When the sunlight comes through smoky clouds or air, it may make everything look rather yellow. Then people say it is a "yellow" day.

Dust in clouds adds to the beautiful cloud colors

when the sun shines against them. The most gorgeous colors in the sky at sunrise or sunset may be due largely to the dust in the air. Sometimes dust from volcanoes stays in the air for months and causes red sunsets all that time.

We must look up to see most clouds if we are on low ground. If we climb to a mountain top, we may pass through a cloud. We may climb higher than the cloud and then look down to see it. People who ride in airplanes or airships often go through clouds or above them.

How would you like to be in a cloud? Do you know how the air would seem then? Could you see very well? You do not always need to climb a mountain or ride in an airplane to get into a cloud. Some clouds are so low that they may touch the ground.

Fog, you know, is a name that we give to cloud vapor that is low. The tiny misty water particles in fog are often so close together that we can see only a little way. The pilot who steers a ship dreads a thick fog. A person who drives an automobile through a heavy fog needs to go very slowly indeed. Travelers, by sea or by land, are often in danger during foggy weather.

Fogs, however, may give pleasure in some ways. When they are not too thick, we can see objects through them in a dim light. A tree or some other bit of landscape, seen through misty air, may look even more beautiful than it does in bright, clear sunlight. Some artists like to take photographs of things they see through a fog. Other artists like to paint fog pictures.

Winter fog

What To Do after Reading Chapter Twenty-Two

NAMES OF CLOUDS

In most books about clouds Latin words are used for the names of clouds. Would you like to know what three of the most common names are? The Latin word *cirrus* means a *curl*. The Latin word *stratus* means a *spread* (or *layer*). The Latin word *cumulus* means a heap (or *mound*).

Look in different books for cloud pictures. Find at least three forms.

Watch the sky every day until you have seen curly clouds and layer clouds and mound clouds.

Notice whether you find just one kind of cloud in the sky at any time. Do you often find two or more kinds at the same time?

Draw sky pictures with three different forms of clouds. Put a name under each form. Use the English name or the Latin name—as you wish.

CHAPTER XXIII

SUMMER ON A DESERT

Some plants grow in water. The white water lily holds only its floating leaves and blossoms where the sun and air can touch them. All its long stems are under water. Marsh marigolds and water forget-me-nots and many other plants can hold their stems above water though they live where their roots remain in wet ground. Most wild plants that live in grassy fields, away from ponds and streams, need rain enough to keep the soil moist.

Field crops and cultivated garden crops need rain, too. Such plants wither and die if dry weather lasts too long. Then farmers have a hard time. They can grow no crops to sell and no grain for their cattle when there is serious drought.

There are plants, however, that can stand long dry seasons. They can keep their health in spite of droughts. Indeed, they could not live in moist climates. They would perish if anyone planted them in a marsh. Such plants can be found in desert places.

Of course even desert plants need some moisture. No plants can grow in the very driest parts of the world.

Giant cactus

But all desert plants can live through long dry spells and thrive in climates where drought lasts most of the year. In many deserts enough rain falls to keep some kinds of plants alive. Heavy dews often help, too.

Different kinds of desert plants have different ways of standing dry weather.

You know that some plants in cold climates spend the winter in the seed stage. That is the way some desert plants spend a season of drought. They remain in the seed stage while the soil is too dry for any young roots to start. During the short rainy season they sprout and grow very fast and have seeds. Then their seeds rest through the next dry season.

Most trees and bushes that live where the winters are cold shed their leaves in the fall and have bare branches until spring. Some desert plants shed their leaves at the close of their growing season and keep their branches bare during the long drought.

Cacti (or cactuses) are plants that have other ways of getting along in dry places. There are many kinds of cacti. Most of them are leafless all through the year. Even though they have no leaves, they can make sugar and starch as well as plants with green leaves can. A cactus keeps the green-colored substance in its fleshy stem. Its sugar factory is in its stem instead of in leaves.

Some cacti have jointed stems. The joints may be of different shapes. Those of the Christmas cactus are shaped like fleshy leaves. People often have these cacti in their homes. They call them Christmas cacti because they blossom in December. Many cacti have barrel-shaped stems.

Trees and other leafy plants lose a great deal of water. The water is given off from their leaves in the form of vapor. Giving up vapor does plants no harm if they can get all the water they need with their roots. But desert plants cannot spare so much water. Cacti must save as much water as they can. Their roots absorb it from the soil during the brief rainy season. They store it in their stems. The water does not go off in vapor from the surface of the green stems as it would through the pores in leaves. So a big thick cactus keeps its barrels

In March when the Mohave Desert is covered with blossoms

of water in its own body. Then it does not become too thirsty and wilt during the dry seasons.

The watery pulp in a cactus is sweet like sweet sap. Many animals like the taste of it. They like it so well that, when they are thirsty, they might eat all these juicy plants if they could. Then there would be no desert cacti. It is fortunate for the wild good-tasting cacti that they are protected. They have spines to take care of them. Their bodies are covered with spines so sharp that they hurt any animal that touches them. In that way they save their own lives and keep the water they need.

Flower and fruit of prickly pear

Men cultivate a kind of cactus called the prickly pear. They grow it as a crop in dry fields. They burn off the spines with torches, and then their cattle can eat the juicy food. The fruit of the prickly pear is sweet and juicy, too. People in Mexico and many other places like to eat it. When the fruit is ripe, it is easy to rub off the

201

spines in the sand or to wash them off in water.

Animals, as well as plants, can live in deserts and semideserts. (*Semi* means *half.*) Of course all kinds cannot live in these dry climates. They must have bodies

Prickly pears have no leaves.
They have broad, flat, jointed stems.

of the right sort to stand the drought. And their habits must be suited to their surroundings.

Horned lizards are good examples of animals that can live in deserts. Some people call them horned toads, because their bodies are somewhat toad-shaped. But they are really lizards. The upper parts of their bodies are pretty well covered by little horns.

A horned lizard

A horned lizard can live in places where the sun beats down on the dry sand. It does not mind the hottest summer day. It does not need to rest in the shade but darts about after food. It likes ants and beetles and caterpillars and other insects. It likes spiders, too. It hunts only during the hottest part of the day and goes to bed early, before the air grows cool.

Before sunset the horned lizard pokes its nose into the warm sand and shoves it along like a little plow. When it has made a shallow bed for itself, it flattens its body and throws sand over itself with its horny sides. Sometimes it leaves its head sticking out in the air. At other times it tucks itself, head and all, under cover. There it waits until the heat of the next day's sun calls it to breakfast.

About fifteen kinds of horned lizards live in southwestern parts of the United States.

What To Do after Reading Chapter Twenty-Three

DESERTLIKE PLACES

When we speak of deserts, we usually mean places where little rain falls. Lack of rain, however, is not the only reason why a place may be a desert.

A desert may be a place where the ground is frozen so much of the year that few or no plants can grow there.

On the seashore rocks are pounded into sand by the waves. The sand is pushed up on the beach. At low tide, when the sand is dry, some of it may be blown inland by heavy winds. Places called sand dunes have been made in this manner. Such sand dunes are like deserts or semideserts in many ways.

Tell how each of the places named below may be desertlike in some ways. Tell what makes it so.

(1) A gravel walk in a dooryard or a park

(2) A sand bank or a gravel pit

(3) A sand or gravel road

(4) An outdoor sand pile where children play

(5) A playground in a school yard or a park

Visit a place like one of those just mentioned. See if you can find any plants growing on them or at their edges. If so, find out what sort of plants they are. Find out, if you can, why the plants are fitted to grow in such a place.

Sand dunes at the seashore

Look for the word *desert* in the index of *First Lessons in Geography* and *Introduction to World Geography*. Then find the right pages and read what is written about deserts in these two books.

Perhaps you call it a toadstool.

CHAPTER XXIV

PLANTS WITH NO GREEN COLOR

Sugar is a necessary food for all plants. All plants with green leaves can make starch for themselves, and the starch can be changed to sugar. Leafless cacti can make sugar in their green stems. But no plant without green color can make sugar and starch.

As you know, a plant with roots absorbs water from the soil. This water has nitrates or other foods dissolved in it. But a mushroom, for example, has no roots. How can it get food? Since it cannot make sugar and starch—for it has no green color—and since it cannot get food with roots, it must have some other way.

Mushrooms, you may remember, use food that other living things have prepared. Sugar has been put into such food. It may be in a changed form, but it is still good food for mushrooms. Some of these leafless plants find their food in the roots of dead trees or in old tree stumps. Some find food in old damp brown leaves or other humus in the soil. Instead of roots, a mushroom has whitish *fungus threads*. These threads run through the humus or other substance on which they feed. They absorb food from these substances.

A mushroom has another part besides the fungus threads. This other part is the fruit body. The fruit body is the part of the mushroom we usually see above ground. There are no seeds, such as flowering plants have, in the fruit body. Instead, there are thousands or millions of spores. The spores, which are, you know, finer than most dust, are blown about by the wind. Some of them come to rest in places where they can find what they need. Then they grow into fungus threads. Later the fruit bodies appear.

Puffballs growing on an old log in the woods

Mushrooms have different kinds of fruit bodies. Some are ball-shaped. The balls are filled with threads and spores. At first they are a firm and white mass. Later they look as if they had yellow or brown stains. At last the contents of the ball become a powdery dark mixture of ripe spores and broken dry threads. By this time the outer case of the ball looks like a brown skin. When this tears, the powder comes puffing out like smoke. We call mushrooms of this sort *puffballs*. A single puffball may have millions and millions of spores.

You may sometimes find puffballs that are as small as the tip of your thumb. Some kinds grow bigger than your head. Children usually like to kick ripe puffballs to see the powder come puffing out. But they do not like to get the dust in their eyes.

The fruit bodies of some mushrooms have shelf-shaped or cap-shaped or saucer-shaped tops. Attached to the under side of the tops there may be many thin strips that grow in rows. They look a little like the edges of the pages of a partly open book. These thin parts are

Gill mushrooms

called *gills*. They bear the spores. Mushrooms with gills are called *gill mushrooms*.

A young spore body of a gill mushroom is not shaped like a fully grown one. At first it is a whitish rounded lump. It is called a *button* then. The button, or very young gill mushroom, looks rather like a little puffball.

Young gill mushrooms (buttons)

Many mushrooms with shelf-shaped or cap-shaped or saucer-shaped tops do not have gills. Instead, they have little tubes crowded close together. Their spores grow in these tubes. Each tube has an open end. This tiny opening is called a *pore*. Mushrooms with pores are called *pore* mushrooms. A young pore mushroom, or button, often resembles a small puffball.

There are hundreds and hundreds of kinds of mushrooms that are good to cook and eat while they are firm and fresh. There are some kinds that are poisonous enough to make a person ill. There are a few kinds that have so much deadly poison in them that a small piece of one mushroom is enough to kill a person.

Pore mushrooms

Some pore mushrooms are good to eat. Some are poisonous. Some gill mushrooms are delicious and harmless. Some are deadly. Puffballs are good to cook and eat while they are firm and white inside. If you could always be sure of getting a real puffball, there would be no danger in gathering these. However, the young buttons of poisonous gill mushrooms and pore mushrooms look so much like small puffballs that they are often mistaken for them.

People who study mushrooms carefully learn how to tell the poisonous kinds from the edible, or eatable, kinds. Some of the edible gill mushrooms look so much like the most deadly kinds that it is not safe for anyone to gather them unless he has learned to tell them apart. It is quite easy to forget the differences. So you will understand why it is not safe for children to gather mushrooms to eat. When you are older, you may wish to learn more about the different kinds.

You may have noticed how rapidly the fruit bodies of some of these large fungi grow. Perhaps you will find a group of toadstools standing in a shady place where there was nothing of that sort a few days before. A few days later you may find that these forms have fallen in soft sloppy pieces and lie spoiling on the ground.

Bracket fungus

All fungi do not appear and perish so quickly. Some of the *bracket fungi* live for many years. Such bracket fungi grow out like shelves on the sides of trees. Many of them live only on old stumps or other dead wood. Some, however, grow from wounds in a living tree—their fungus threads push their way into the growing parts of the tree and damage it.

After the fungus threads have been growing for some time in the wood, the fruit body of the fungus pushes out at the side. The first year it is a very small shelf with pores on its under surface. The next year a new layer grows across the under side and reaches a little beyond it to make a wider shelf. A new layer grows in this way each year for a long time. Each season the crowded tubes grow in the new layer and the spores come out of the open pores of these tubes. Because of the way these layers are formed, the bracket is thickest near the tree and thin at its outer edge. Bracket fungi are tough like wood or leather. They sometimes grow more than fifty years. Some day, perhaps, you may find such a fungus that is older than your grandfather.

The fungi you have read about so far in this chapter have been of large kinds. There are fungi, however, so small that you cannot see them unless you look at them through a magnifying glass. The kind of fungus that causes late blight in potatoes, you remember, is as small as this.

The tiny fungi are not shaped like gill mushrooms and pore mushrooms. They have their own kinds of fruit bodies with spores. Some have very fine, delicate fungus threads that grow through the substances which they use for food.

Yeast, which is used in making "raised" bread, is a kind of fungus that thrives in dough. As it grows it forms little bubbles of gas that make the dough "rise." The holes in the bread are the places where the gas made bubbles in the dough. The gas is driven out of these

213

Rust on barberry leaves

holes by the heat. The heat also kills the yeast fungi in the bread.

Many kinds of small fungi are helpful in the world, because they live in old fallen leaves and help them decay. If it were not for such fungi, the fallen leaves year by year would be piled in enormous heaps that would be in the way of everything else.

Some kinds of small fungi do not wait until leafy plants have shed their leaves to use them. They take food from living leaves and other parts of the green plants. This is bad for the plants, as they cannot then keep well.

Plant doctors sometimes say that certain plants are sick with a *rust*. A rust is a fungus with spores that are about the same color as the bright brown dust that may be seen on rusty iron.

Blight diseases are also caused by fungi. Besides potato plants, which have late blight, you know, certain other plants have fungus blights.

There are so many fungi in the world that some of their spores are always near us. If you rub your finger across a dusty table or chair or desk, you will probably get some fungus spores on your finger. Perhaps they will be the spores of an interesting kind of mold, for molds, you remember, are fungus plants.

What To Do after Reading Chapter Twenty-Four

GROWING SOME MOLD

Choose some material that will make a good home for mold to grow in. If you cannot think what to take, any of the following will do:

(1) A brown leaf that fell from a tree last fall

(2) A slice of brown bread or white bread

(3) A few boiled or baked beans

(4) Slices of boiled or baked potato

(5) A little fruit sauce or jelly

Divide into 4 parts each kind of material you choose for your experiment. Put each part in a saucer and have a glass to cover it.

Place 2 of the parts in a hot oven until they are dry. (Do not have them covered while they are in the oven.) Then keep these dry parts in a dry, sunny place.

Keep 2 parts moist. Leave them in a warm, dark place.

Find dust on a window sill or furniture or some other dusty place. Rub your finger or a bit of cloth over the dust. Then touch 1 dry part and 1 moist part with your finger or dusty cloth.

Look at all 4 parts every few days.

Tell whether mold grows on all 4 parts.

WILD YEAST

You have doubtless seen cakes of the yeast that is commonly used to cause homemade bread to rise. You may know, too, that bakers use yeast, though they keep it in a soft condition and do not have it pressed into firm cakes.

Perhaps, however, you do not know that it is not necessary to put prepared yeast into dough to make it rise. Wild yeast will get into various substances by itself and grow in them if it is given a chance.

A yeast plant has one simple part, or cell. In this respect yeast plants are like bacteria. Tiny yeast cells float about in the air as bacteria do. Such yeast is called wild yeast.

If you wish to give some wild-yeast plants a chance to grow, you can do this as follows:

Scald 1 cup of milk. Let it cool until it is lukewarm. Then stir into it 1 tablespoon of sugar, 1 teaspoon of salt, and 2 tablespoons of white corn meal. Pour this mixture into a pitcher or fruit jar. Place the uncovered pitcher or jar in water as hot as you can put your hand into without pain. (Half boiling water and half cold water from a faucet will be about right.) Let your mixture stand undisturbed for six or seven hours, or until the yeast plants are causing bubbles of gas to form. If you listen, you can hear the sound the gas causes as it moves.

By this time you will have enough wild yeast for a

loaf of bread. If you wish to make the bread, it is time to stir a cupful of flour into your mixture and let it rise. You will then need to ask some one who knows how to make ordinary bread to tell you how to prepare your stiff dough and when to bake it.

CHAPTER XXV

SOUR SOIL

There was once a man who tried to grow blueberry bushes in ordinary garden soil. He said he thought people could have cultivated blueberries as well as other cultivated fruit. So he planted some in rows, as he did raspberries and blackberries. He made the soil rich with food that would have agreed very well with rosebushes. Then he waited to see what would happen. He was experimenting with blueberries.

That man's blueberry bushes did not thrive. They did not grow nearly so well as they had grown while they were wild. The fruit was small. The bushes had had much better berries before they were planted in the garden. The bushes lived a few seasons in a feeble sort of way and then died.

Other people experimented with blueberries. Some of them, like the man of whom you have just read, planted the bushes in garden soil where other kinds of plants had flourished. But the more ordinary fertilizers these people gave the bushes for food, the more starved the poor bushes seemed. When they put lime in the soil, the bushes became sicker than ever. So all these

219

A cluster of large blueberries

experimenters thought that blueberries must be very hard to grow as a cultivated crop.

After a while, however, a man decided to make an experiment with a different sort of soil. He took some soil that was so sour it would have disagreed with most kinds of garden plants. It was a soil with peat in it. Peat is composed of partly decayed leaves and other vegetable matter, such as old stems and roots. It is common in bogs. He put this sour, peaty soil into flowerpots and planted some blueberry seeds. After the seeds sprouted, the young plants grew rapidly and were strong and healthy.

As soon as people learned about that experiment and others made with blueberries and sour soil, they stopped trying to grow these bushes in ordinary garden ground.

Now you may find in certain parts of the United States cultivated blueberries that thrive. They are planted carefully and pruned. There are some varieties that have such large berries crowded on their stems they might make you think of bunches of little grapes. If you ever see a box of such fruit for sale in a store, you may be sure it was picked from bushes that live in sour soil.

There is something else that is very interesting about blueberry plants. Their roots are covered with a kind of fungus, but the fungus does them no harm. It does not give the bushes any disease. Indeed, the fungus helps the blueberry roots and the blueberry roots help the fungus. They have a strange sort of partnership.

The blueberry roots give the fungus a favorable place

Picking cultivated blueberries

to grow. They share with it some of their food made from sugar. In return the fungus helps the blueberry roots get nitrogen food. Nitrogen is not easy to take from sour soil without such help.

How can you tell whether soil is sour (acid) or not? You can tell that lemon juice or a cranberry is acid by tasting it. It would be rather unpleasant to test soil by chewing it!

You may have heard of a dye called litmus. Paper dyed with litmus is pink or red if it is dipped in an acid liquid. It is blue if it is dipped in an *alkaline* liquid. An *alkali* is a mineral that destroys acid. Lime is one kind of alkali. Soil is said to be alkaline if it has much lime or other alkali in it. A sample of soil may be stirred in water and tested with litmus paper.

The litmus test is the simplest way of finding out whether soil is acid. There are other tests that people use when they need to know exactly how acid the soil is. One chemical they use for such a test has a name with fifteen letters in it. As this name is rather hard to pronounce and remember, perhaps you will be satisfied with the litmus test for the present.

Of course many kinds of plants do not thrive on acid soil. People often put lime on the ground in their gardens. Farmers scatter lime on their meadows if the grass is not growing well enough to make a good hay crop. Lime reduces the amount of acid in the soil. If enough is used, it will change all the acid. Then the soil becomes alkaline.

Some peat land is not acid. In certain places there

are springs or ponds with alkaline water near the peat. Such water makes all the peat it touches alkaline, too.

Plowing sour soil for a blueberry plantation

If you were going to choose a place for a blueberry plantation, you might not need to test the soil. There is another way you could know about it. If wild blueberries are growing there, you will know the ground is sour. If cranberries are there, you will know, too, because cranberries live in acid soil. That is the way men often choose places to put their cultivated blueberries. They hunt for land that has wild blueberries or cranberries growing on it. Then they clear off the trees and bushes that are there and plow the ground for a blueberry plantation.

What To Do after Reading Chapter Twenty-Five

SOUR SOIL AND SOIL WITH LIME

Here are suggestions for two experiments.

Choose one of them and make it, if you can. If you cannot do one of these, think of some other experiment to test soil.

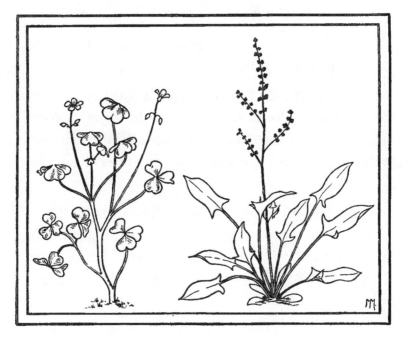

Wood sorrel and field sorrel

Experiment I. Visit a greenhouse. Find some little weeds called wood sorrel.[2] Ask the person in charge of the greenhouse to give you a few of these weeds. Buy a little of the soil in which they are growing—enough

[2]Oxalis.

for two small pots or boxes.

Test the soil to see whether it is acid. (Use the litmus test.)

Fill one pot or box with the soil and plant a wood sorrel in it. Do not add any lime to this soil.

If you find the soil is acid, put lime in enough soil for one pot or box. Use 100 parts of soil to 1 part of lime. Mix the lime well with the soil, moisten it, and do not use it for several days. Then plant a wood sorrel in it.

Watch the two wood sorrels for a few weeks. Which one seems the healthier?

Experiment II. Take a walk in a country field or a city park. Look for wood sorrel or field sorrel[3] or bluets. Ask if you may have a little of the soil in which some of these plants are growing. Ask if you may have a few of the plants.

Test the soil to see if it is acid. Use some of the soil as it is. Add lime to some. Put some of your plants in the untreated soil. Put some in the soil to which you have added lime. Watch to see which plants thrive better.

[3]Rumex.

CHAPTER XXVI

SOME HARMLESS SNAKES

Did you ever watch a snake glide gracefully across a rock and slip quickly into some hole? Snakes (or serpents, as they are also called) are so very timid that they do not remain where you can see them unless you are very careful not to frighten them.

In another chapter in this book you read about a boy named William Hudson. You may remember that he often saw deer and flamingos and parrots and rheas. He did not need to visit a zoo to see them, for he found them all on the pampas of South America.

He watched snakes on the pampas, too; and when he went to England to live he watched snakes there. The more he saw of them, the better he liked them. He became so much interested in them, indeed, that he planned to write a book about them. He thought a good name for it would be *The Book of the Serpent*. He never got that book written, but he did write several chapters about snakes. These chapters have been printed in some of his other books. If you are interested in snakes yourself, you may enjoy reading what William Hudson wrote about them. But you will understand his thoughts better if you wait until you are much older before you read them.

You may have heard of Solomon. He was a son of a man named David, and he ruled over a land called Israel. That was a long time ago—more than twenty-eight hundred years ago. Solomon was so wise that people still like to quote some of his words. He said that the way of a serpent upon a rock was too wonderful for him to know.

In those days no one understood how a serpent

could go so easily without any feet. It was a mystery to everybody. People wondered for thousands of years how a snake could walk. At last some one studied to see how the body of a snake is formed inside as well as outside. Since then there has not been so much mystery about its motions.

Perhaps you, too, have wondered how a snake can travel swiftly and smoothly. It moves with more grace than animals that have feet. Would you like to understand how it manages to glide in its own strange way? Do you think it would be rather jolly to learn something about snakes that even Solomon did not know?

A snake's body is covered with scales. The scales are small on its back and sides. But the under scales are long. They reach sidewise across the under side of the body and look like a row of even strips.

You know that your backbone is a row of connected movable short bones. These bones are called *vertebrae*. (Each one is a *vertebra*.) Do you know how many vertebrae you have? A snake has more than you have— some kinds have nearly three hundred vertebrae.

A snake has more ribs than you have, too. Nearly every vertebra of a snake has a pair of ribs or riblike bones attached to it. The snake can wiggle these bones as easily as you can wiggle your fingers.

Near the tip of each rib there are muscles that connect with one end of an under scale. So when a pair of ribs moves, an under scale moves, too. That is the way a snake walks. It creeps with the tips of its ribs.

The under scales, which are moved by the ribs, pass over the ground or any ordinary rough surface. They go with a rippling motion.

Notice the shape of the under scales.

A snake cannot creep on smooth glass. Such glass has no roughness for the under scales to cling to or push against. But of course a snake would not be likely to find anything so smooth as glass in the places where he lives.

At regular times (once a year or oftener) a snake molts his outer, scaly skin. He sheds even the coating of his eyes. Just before he molts he is nearly blind. At other times his eyes are bright. They are always wide open, for he has no eyelids at all.

A snake's ears do not show. They have no openings on the outside of his head. He has some rather feeble organs of hearing inside his head, but they are not much good to him. He does not need ears, however, for he hears with his delicate forked tongue.

You know that every sound comes from a sound wave, or a vibration, in the air. A snake's tongue is so sensitive it can feel the sound vibrations. That is the reason why a snake sticks out his tongue when he is startled. He is listening with it to find out where the danger is. He cannot "sting" with his tongue or hurt anything with it.

Perhaps you have been taught to be afraid of snakes. There are, indeed, some kinds of snakes with fangs, or dangerous teeth. The fangs are connected with glands filled with deadly poison. When such a snake bites with its fangs, the poison pours into the wound. If there are rattlesnakes or other snakes with poison fangs in your part of the country, you should of course keep safely away from them. But there is no reason whatever why you should avoid such harmless kinds as look very different.

Would you like to learn how to know some snakes that are safe as well as interesting to watch? There are many harmless serpents, but the kinds you are most likely to meet are ribbon snakes and garter snakes and green snakes.

A ribbon snake might make you think of a piece of

dark ribbon with three pretty stripes. The stripes run the long way of the body, from head to tail. Two are side stripes and the third one runs along the middle of the back. They are usually yellow or orange and they are often very bright. Some kinds of ribbon snakes live in boggy or marshy places. They like small toads and frogs to eat, and they go into the water for tadpoles.

A ribbon snake

Garter snakes are striped snakes, too, and they are closely related to ribbon snakes. Most of them are not quite so slender and graceful as ribbon snakes, and their yellow stripes are not quite so bright. Common garter snakes may be found in swamps, in woods, in meadows, and on hillsides. They like frogs and toads and earthworms to eat and they spend much of their time hunting.

A mother ribbon or garter snake does not lay her eggs. She keeps them in her body until they hatch. Then the young snakes are born. These baby snakes can creep and hunt for their very first dinner, but their mother stays near to protect them while they are young.

Garter snake taking a sun bath

Green snakes are dainty little serpents. They live near meadows and often hide under stone heaps. They are leaf green in color. It is not easy to see them in grassy places. They like to eat grasshoppers and smooth caterpillars and some other insects. They eat spiders, too; but they do not care for earthworms. Mother green snakes lay their eggs before they hatch.

You may have met people who scream when they see a serpent—even a dainty little green snake! They shudder if they hear anyone speak of a serpent—even a harmless and pretty ribbon snake! Perhaps you like to scream and shudder, too, at such times.

Perhaps, however, the more you know about snakes,

A green snake

the better you will like them. That was what happened
to William Hudson. Indeed, many people find these
animals so interesting that they enjoy watching them
to learn their habits. Like Solomon, so many years ago,
they find the ways of the serpent exceedingly wonderful.
There is a man who knows a great deal about snakes—
perhaps as much as anyone else in the world. He is not
ashamed to say that his "favorite creature in Nature has,
from early boyhood days, been *the serpent.*"

What To Do after Reading Chapter Twenty-Six

LOOK AT REPTILE PICTURES

There is a class of animals called *reptiles*. Turtles, crocodiles, alligators, lizards, and snakes are all reptiles.

Would you like to know the name of the man who said that the serpent is his "favorite creature in Nature"? His name is Raymond L. Ditmars. He has written some books about reptiles. There are excellent pictures of snakes and other reptiles in these books. Visit a library and ask to see one of these books. Look at the pictures of the different kinds of reptiles.

Put your hand, or a piece of paper, over all of a turtle picture except its head. Do you think that the head of the turtle looks rather like that of a snake?

Does a crocodile look more like a turtle, a lizard, or a snake? In what ways are the two alike?

What do turtles have that snakes and lizards lack? What do snakes lack that turtles and lizards have?

READ

Read one or more of the following selections:

(1) "The Painted Turtle," a chapter in *Holiday Pond*.

(2) "Sir Talis," a chapter in *Holiday Hill*.

(3) Read about three kinds of reptiles in *First Lessons in Nature Study*: Read about a lizard in Chapter 14, snakes in Chapter 5, and a turtle in Chapter 11.

WRITE

"What I Saw a Reptile Do." If you have ever seen a live reptile free or in a zoo, write about it.

"A Reptile I Should Like to See." If you have never seen a live reptile, write about one you would like to watch.

Turn to page 228 of this book. Notice that no title (name) or description is printed under the picture on that page. Think of a good title for that picture. Write your title on a piece of paper. Then write a paragraph telling whether or not you would be smiling if you were doing what the girl in the picture is doing.

CHAPTER XXVII

HUNTING FOR BOULDERS

Have you a collection of stones? Many boys and girls like to pick up samples of rocks they find outdoors. Some kinds, too, can be bought for very little. A piece of chalk, a lump of coal, a bit of slate, a pretty round agate (used in playing marbles), and some other kinds can be purchased in stores by children who do not live near mines or quarries or any stony country places.

It is really very interesting to make a collection of stones and learn facts about each kind. The true stories of all stones are marvelous in one way or another. But perhaps no stone has a stranger story than a boulder.

Some boulders are so small you could carry them in your pocket. Some are so huge they weigh many tons. But, large or small, they all have had much the same sort of time in the world. They have all gone on journeys. They all found the traveling very rough. They were broken and rubbed while they were going from place to place. Their corners and sharp edges were ground off. That is why they have rounded shapes.

How did these rocks travel? They rode with glaciers! You already know something about glaciers. In the

Granite boulder

chapter called "White Crystals" you learned that they are formed by deep masses of snow that fell flake by flake for years and years on cold mountains. The snow becomes so heavy it presses together in ice. Enormous bodies of such ice move slowly down the mountain sides, grinding and crushing everything they touch.

A grinding glacier breaks off some of the rocks of the mountain. These become embedded in the moving mass of ice and are carried along with it. Their journey is very slow—sometimes not more than an inch a day. In time, however, they may reach a place where the ice melts. Then the boulders are at the end of their journey. Their ride in the glacier is over.

Where would you go to look for boulders? Would you go where you can find melting glaciers? Do you think Glacier National Park would be a good place? Would you go to the northern seashore, where glaciers crack into icebergs?

It would be interesting to visit those places. You could doubtless find boulders there. If you went to certain places, you might find boulders that reached their journey's end not more than a thousand years ago. You might find some that had been left there a hundred years ago—or perhaps not even so long ago as that.

But you do not really need to visit melting glaciers to find boulders. There are plenty of them hundreds of miles from the nearest glacier. In the western part of North America you may find boulders all the way from Alaska to California. In the northern and eastern parts of the United States there are boulders scattered

A glacier in Beartooth National Forest, Montana

over the states between the Ohio and the Missouri rivers; there are boulders as far south as New Jersey and Pennsylvania; and there are millions of boulders in New York and the New England states.

So if you live in any of these places, you can have a boulder hunt almost any day that you can spend in the country. Of course the boulders stay there all the year round, but you will have more time to look for them during your summer vacation. You may not need to search very long. Perhaps the very first stone you climb over will be a boulder!

Do you think it strange to have a boulder hunt where there are no glaciers? Scientists once thought it was very queer indeed that there could be great and little granite stones, round as pebbles, all over the northeastern United States and in southern Canada. It was like a puzzle to them. The scientists studied the granite stones. Some of them were the same sort of granite as the sides of mountains hundreds of miles away. They thought the pieces of granite had been brought from those mountains. But how did they get scattered all about—thousands and millions and billions of them? At last an answer to the puzzle was found.

A boulder in Glacier National Park

The answer is that once long, long ago all these places were covered with moving ice. One great field of ice covered much of Canada and the northeastern part of the United States. It was very heavy, for it was several thousand feet thick in some places.

The answer to the boulder puzzle explains many other matters, too. The mountains and hills in this same part of the continent have rounded tops. That is partly because they were ground down by the mighty glaciers that moved across them.

New England hills have rounded tops.

The valleys are wide—much wider than their rivers of water have ever made them. They are so wide because mighty glacial rivers of ice and rocks once came crushing through them.

The very soil in this part of the continent is peculiar. It is made of rocks that have been ground to bits. Some of it was left rather coarse and full of gravel. Some of it was ground until it became as fine as powder. Some of the powder was formed into clay, called *boulder clay* because there are so many boulders in it.

A valley

So when you go for a boulder hunt some summer, you may walk in a broad valley where once a glacier went. You may climb a hill that had its top rubbed down by drifting ice. You may find rocks with grooves in them where old glaciers scraped. Such marks are called *glacial scratches*. You may come to a lake that was started many years before by a melting glacier.

Of course all this took place long, long ago. Just how long no one knows. We speak of that time as the *Glacial Period* or the *Ice Age*. Men who have studied the boulder-glacier puzzle carefully and know most about it think that the Ice Age must have lasted at least 500,000 years. They think that it was at least 25,000 years ago since the last of this ice disappeared in the northern United States.

When you find a boulder, you may think what a rough ride it had once upon a time. You may think, too, how very quietly it has been resting for thousands of years since then.

What To Do after Reading Chapter Twenty-Seven

HUNT FOR BOULDERS, COBBLES, PEBBLES, SAND, AND GRAVEL

You have learned a little about boulders (sometimes written *bowlders* or *bolders*). Boulders may be large or small, but the name is usually given to rather large rocks the edges of which have been rubbed and worn.

The name *cobble* is given to a stone that has been rubbed smooth by moving water. Small cobbles may be called *pebbles* or *gravel*. Very fine pieces of crushed or crumbled rocks are called *sand*.

Look for pieces of worn stone that are of different sizes, from those as big as large boulders to those as small as sand. Learn as much as you can about what you find. Then write or tell what you learn.

(1) *Boulders.* Where did you find a boulder? Was it in a park where some one had put it? Did it have letters cut in its side? Was it a sort of stone monument?

Did you find boulders in a stone wall? Why had they been put there? Where were they before they were put into the wall?

Did you find a boulder in a shaded woody place? Was there moss growing on the boulder near the ground? Were there ferns (the kind called rock ferns) growing with a thick mat of roots on the top of the boulder?

(2) *Cobbles*. Did you find cobbles? Were they used for a stone wall or were they lying on the ground? Were they at the seashore? Were they at the edge of a river or brook? What had given them their rounded shape?

Why are these stones smooth with rounded edges?

(3) *Pebbles*. Where did you find some pebbles? Had any person put them there to use? Were they near some cobbles? What colors were they?

(4) *Sand*. Did you ever play in a sand pile? Do you know where your sand came from? Was it from a seashore? Was it from a sand bank? Was it from the shore of a lake?

(5) *Gravel.* Did you see men using a mixture of pebbles and sand that they called gravel? What were they doing with it? Where did they get it?

READ

Read "The Old Boulder," a chapter in *Holiday Hill.*

A BOULDER STORY

Write, or tell, a story of what you think might have happened to a granite boulder.

Start your story by telling of what the granite was a part before it became a boulder. Explain what broke off the piece of granite and changed it to a boulder.

You may choose a western or an eastern boulder for your story. Tell through what parts of North America your boulder traveled and name the state in which it came to rest at last. (You may look at a globe or at other maps.) Explain what carried the boulder from place to place and why it stopped after moving for many, many years. Explain why no one could watch it during its journey.

CHAPTER XXVIII

THE LAST DAY OF SUMMER

If you look for the word *summer* in one dictionary, you may read that it is "the hottest or warmest season of the year, including June, July, and August in the northern *hemisphere*." (*Hemi* means *half*, and *sphere* is *globe*. The northern hemisphere is the northern half of the earth.) So you might think that August 31 would be the last day of summer for those who live north of the *equator!* (The equator, you know, is the great circle around the earth's surface halfway between the poles.) Look on your schoolroom globe for a line which shows where the equator is. Of course on the real earth there is no line to mark the equator circle.

In another dictionary you may read that summer "in the United States is reckoned as the months June, July, and August; in Great Britain as May, June, and July." So if you invited a friend in England to spend the summer with you, your guest might arrive the very first of May!

But if you read about the seasons in a science book that tells of planets, our sun, and other stars and their motions, what do you learn? You will be told in such a

247

A day in summer

book (on *astronomy*) that autumn begins on September 23 in the northern hemisphere. So that would make September 22 the last day of summer!

Rather puzzling, isn't it? How is anyone to know when summer really begins and ends?

Many words are used in more than one way. Such a word may have a common everyday meaning and a special scientific meaning. *Summer* is a word that may be used in different ways. It is the common custom in the United States and Canada to call June, July, and August the summer months. In this sense the summer begins June 1 and ends August 31. It is quite correct to use the word in this way for ordinary purposes. But if you are talking about the four seasons in a scientific way, you will need to think differently about the time when summer or any other season begins and ends.

You have learned that the earth moves around the sun once in a year. You know that the earth is turned so that the north pole points toward the North Star all through the year. So while the earth is traveling in a circle around the sun, the sunlight does not touch the earth in just the same way at different times. Thus we have more hours of sunlight during some times of the year and more hours of darkness at other times.

There are four days each year when the sun and the earth are in positions of special importance. Those days are March 21, June 21, September 23, and December 21. You read about those days in Chapter Thirteen of this book. Do you remember why we call those days the beginnings of the four seasons? If you have forgotten, you might read that chapter again. Then you will see again what day is the last day of summer if you are using the word in a *scientific* sense.

When you get used to the two ways of speaking about the seasons, you will find it easy to tell which is meant. You can keep the two ways clear in your mind when you say that one kind of summer ends August 31 and the other kind ends September 22.

And now that we have reached the end of summer, it will be a good time to end this book, for in its pages we have gone through the four seasons of fall, winter, spring, and summer.

School days

What To Do after Reading Chapter Twenty-Eight

YOUR FAVORITE SEASON

Talk about the four seasons. Divide your class into four parties. Let each party talk about one season. Tell in what ways each season is different from the others. Tell what you like best to see and do in each season.

Write about one or more of the seasons. Write prose or verse, as you prefer. If you write verse, have at least as many rhyming words as you find in the following stanzas:

MY FAVORITE SEASON

My favorite season is springtime, I think,
When apple-tree boughs are all flowery pink!

Or perhaps I like winter and chickadees best
While slumbering woodchucks and bumblebees rest!

But of course the fall's jolly. Its colors are gay.
I'll never forget one bright autumn day!

And summer? Well, really, I like that best, too. For I
find the year pleasant—all the way through!

A BOOK LIST

Selections from several books have been suggested in connection with the exercises for the different chapters. Here is a list of the books to which such reference has been made.

Bird Stories, by Edith M. Patch.

First Lessons in Geography, by Philip A. Knowlton.

First Lessons in Nature Study, by Edith M. Patch.

Hexapod Stories, by Edith M. Patch.

Holiday Hill, by Edith M. Patch.

Holiday Meadow, by Edith M. Patch.

Holiday Pond, by Edith M. Patch.

Introduction to World Geography, by Philip A. Knowlton.

Nature Narratives, Volume I, by Austin H. Clark.

Surprises by Edith M. Patch and Harrison E. Howe.

CPSIA information can be obtained
at www.ICGtesting.com
Printed in the USA
BVHW070632140720
583600BV00001B/85

9 781633 341029